Dear Chad,
I am grateful for all the
great memories at Santaquin
Elementary. I am looking
forward for many more years

TREASURE YOUR
MOMENTS

at Apple Valley.

A MOMENT IN YOUR HAND

(11) Patty Garcia

ROSIE MARTINEZ

gelato
publishing

Enjoy every moment,
it is a tresure!

Rosie Martinez

3-27-2018

To my husband Ade, my children Oliver, Leah, DD and Shayla with whom I dream to continue living this moment until the eternities.

INTRODUCTION

My Stories

The years may pass, but they do not take our memories. Colorfast, faded, or possibly distorted, these memories are always in our mind, trying to be shared, ensuring that they will not be forgotten.

This collection of stories is undoubtedly only that: my own memories that I lived with the people who I love the most or with the ones that I shared some stages in my life. I want to share this compilation of experiences for one sole purpose, to show that everyone is surrounded by inspiration in their lives, and that even the moments that we considered insignificant or challenging are full of enlightenment. But above all, they are moments that endure and mark our lives to mold us into whom we are today.

We all come to this life to write a story. The date on the first page may be different for everyone, but the beginning is similar because we were all born! Although each life is developed in a different scenario, we all want to finish it with a chapter where our goal of happiness is achieved.

I have learned that even though we have shared the same experiences with family, friends, or acquaintances, we remember them in a different way. Maybe we were in the same place, but the circumstances or conversation did not affect us equally. Maybe we didn't pay attention to details, or we believe that we never participated in that event.

Whatever the circumstances, these are *my* stories. Perhaps some lack a few details or have been painted with exaggeration, but without a doubt, they are infused with love and gratitude for the opportunity to have lived them.

~Rosie Martinez

1

WE ALL NEED FIVE MINUTES

When I was twelve years old, I went to a presentation of the folkloric ballet group in my new school. Each traditional dance displayed not only a sample of the Mexican culture, but also an invitation to show joy. As the dancers' shoes clacked against the wooden floor in almost perfect rhythm, I knew that this was the club I wanted to belong to for the next three years.

Once the program ended, I approached one of the dancers to find out how could I apply to join the group. The girl I asked looked beautiful, even though she used a lot of makeup and fake eyelashes. She smiled and told me that the auditions were going to start the next day after school.

The teacher, a tall, thin, and very nice woman named Luz, welcomed the group of around fifteen girls in the dance room the next afternoon. She explained that there were only four permanent spaces for girls, but those who didn't get accepted could still practice. If during the year someone stopped going, these other girls would have the possibility of taking that place, or surely next year they could become part of the group.

I had never been in a dance group before and for a moment, I thought that it was a great disadvantage, but when she had us make coordinated movements, I realized that it would not be so difficult for me. As the days passed, the number of girls who stayed at the practices became fewer and fewer, and that meant that the chances of staying in the group were greater. Finally, after two weeks, we waited to know the final results. When Luz approached me and said, "You are part of the group," I felt like the happiest girl on the earth.

Of course, I left almost jumping with joy. That same afternoon, I told my parents that I had been accepted, and they were happy about it—until the moment I gave them the list of what I needed. They told me no, because the shoes and the practice suit were too expensive. I explained to them how difficult it had been for me to be chosen, but I could not convince them. They told me that I could possibly dance next year. Although I was discouraged, I continued going to each practice, hoping that their decision would change as the days went by.

At the end of September, the group had another presentation. I didn't dance because I didn't know the dance steps yet, but I was with them backstage, trying to help in any way I could. Nervousness hung in the air as I made sure that the dresses were well-fitted, the shoes did not bother the dancers, and the makeup was enough to be almost seen from the last row of the auditorium. That night, I was convinced that my decision to be part of the group was not a mistake.

Finally, after almost a month of begging my parents every day, they agreed to let me participate. They bought me the shoes a half size too big and the skirt of the suit had to be wrapped around my waist so I would not trip over it. My parents knew that I was going to grow, and they wanted to be sure I would use them for a long time.

A rolled-up skirt with so many folds at the waist made me look not only shorter but fatter. All my friends looked gorgeous in their dresses. They were all slim and tall and had long hair. That was another difficulty I faced: I had short hair and would have to use braids made of yarn. I didn't quite look the same as the rest of my dance team, but I loved dancing, and I was coordinated, so I was chosen to be the leader.

We practiced for many hours every week. Our feet ached and our minds were tired of trying to remember the choreography, but at the end, we received our reward when we were applauded in the presentations.

Eight months later, we had the opportunity to participate in a contest against ten other schools. In a specific number we participated in, I tap danced for a few seconds without music on a small wooden box while my teammates remained silent. To our immense joy, the name of our school was announced as the winner of the contest in the youngest category.

When it was time to receive the trophy, my teacher and my friends decided that I should be the one to receive it. As I walked towards the podium—feeling immense joy at having achieved the honor with my friends what had seemed like a dream until a few minutes before— I heard a girl from another school say, "She dances very well." That comment would have made me grow a little more if I had walked faster, but unfortunately, I heard her mother's voice saying, "Yes, but she is ugly!" At that moment, my happiness and confidence disappeared. I was grateful for all the makeup I was wearing, because nobody saw my sadness, and surely my false eyelashes caught some tears, but I took the trophy, and still I celebrated.

On my way home, my mom asked me why I was sad. I burst into tears when I told her the comment I heard. My mom hugged me and reassured me that I was beautiful, and then she gave me this wise advice: "When you feel upset, when you feel life is unfair or when someone hurts your feelings, take five minutes to scream, to cry, to be sad or mad—but remember, only five minutes. After that, enjoy the rest of the day."

In each stage of my life, I have gone through difficult times. I remember when I found out the boy I liked had a girlfriend and when school grades were not as good as what I expected. I remember realizing that being an adult didn't solve problems but seemed to increase them. I remember the day when the doctor told me that he couldn't hear the heartbeat of the baby I was carrying in my tummy and when my daughter was diagnosed with a rare illness.

In each of these moments, and many more moments after those, I have felt pain, frustration, and anguish. Many times I have felt unable to resolve unpleasant situations that I have had to face, but the words of my mother inspired me to look at the bright side even when challenges arise. After taking five very short minutes of my life to cry, to be sad or upset, I remember that I need to enjoy the rest of my day.

When I look at my husband, I appreciate that the boy I liked had a girlfriend. The challenge to improve in school was always an invitation to get more knowledge. Being an adult has given me the opportunity to go through wonderful experiences. I know that I will have two more children after this life. My daughter, despite her challenges, is alive, and I have had the opportunity not just to share "our five minutes" several times with her, but also many moments full of joy.

I never saw the face of the lady who said I was ugly—that's why I just remember her voice—but I am grateful to her, because her words gave me the opportunity to learn one of the greatest lessons of my life: *There will always be someone or some circumstance that tries to take us away from our days of joy, but the decision to waste or take advantage of the time we have to be happy is only ours.*

2

PINK STORMS

"Forty, forty, forty, here we go, forty! Does anyone want to give more for this beautiful pink stuffed animal that will turn a frown upside down? Fifty, fifty, fifty, there they want it for fifty! Sixty? Seventy?" The auctioneer's voice sounded far away in the middle of so much murmuring, but as I got closer, I heard it more clearly: "Ninety, ninety, ninety!"

I found myself at the auction because I helped serve food. Now my shift was over, so I had an opportunity to approach the auction at the precise moment when the pink stuffed animal was shown again to the audience to increase interest. I observed the stuffed animal and agreed that it was very beautiful.

Without thinking twice, I raised my hand. The auctioneer yelled, "She bids one ten! Does someone want this soft pink dog for one twenty?" Again, I raised my hand, and I knew that I had won it when the same voice said, "Sold!"

At the end of the auction, I felt very happy with my winnings. I held the stuffed animal in my hands and felt how soft it was. I knew I had made a good purchase, not only because of the monetary value, but also for what it represented. When I left the auction I felt tired, yet before I could head home I needed to deliver the pink stuffed animal to someone who would definitely appreciate it.

I met Vicky at a costume party. She was dressed as a pirate, and I felt that the costume suited her perfectly, because her attitude was totally carefree. Her laughter could be heard from anywhere in the room, and it seemed that she knew everyone who arrived. When I approached her corner of the party, she greeted me as if we were lifetime friends. Perhaps I felt like I was in the same boat, as I greeted her in the same way.

Through the years, Vicky and I had the opportunity to get to know each other more. We have shared many experiences, challenges, and sweet moments with each other. However, at some point, we decided to throw the other from our own boat. We both decided that for years we had sailed without the help of the other, so there was no need to stay in the same boat. Even though I missed her laughter and wisdom, I felt that the best thing to do was to set sail on my own.

After a few weeks, I heard that Vicky had been diagnosed with a disease that even the bravest pirate is afraid of. Without thinking twice, I went to see her, and I realized that my journey during our time apart had not been enjoyable. We resumed our friendship as if nothing had happened, and we caught each other up with the latest events in our lives.

During the days when she felt submerged in a sea of sadness, I knew that it was time to throw her a lifesaver so she could have a way to float. My friend had to face several storms, but together we learned that when someone is by our side, those periods of difficulty can be more tolerable and produce less anguish.

On the night of the auction, carrying a pink stuffed animal in my arms, I went to see that pirate who was still fighting bravely to reach a safe harbor where she could throw an anchor to stabilize her life. That night, seeing Vicky hug and sink her face into the softness of the stuffed animal, I learned that only on a few occasions do we have the power to change difficult situations in our lives or of those we love, but the opportunity always exists to offer shelter and protection on that island called friendship. Storms are not only somber when they are gray, but also when they are pink and threaten to return.

3

ARE YOU OK?

The scenery that morning was incredible. While opening the living room window, I caught a glimpse of the flashes of light reflecting on the white sheet that had covered the ground around our home for miles. Prior to that, I had only seen snow in movies or television shows. Without thinking, I opened the door and walked out onto our porch to touch the incredible snow that had fallen to the ground the night before. The moment was almost magical to me.

I grew up in a place where the weather was always warm. I owned a sweater that never had a chance to get worn out. It was pink with pearly white buttons. I used it for a couple of hours on cold mornings and only for a few days each year. I didn't wear my first jacket until I was fifteen years old and left my hometown to study in a city where it was a bit colder. Now I lived in a place where not only the climate was totally different, but also the language.

My husband looked out and told me that I needed to be ready soon. It was Sunday and although I would have loved to continue playing in the snow, it was time to go to church. An hour later, we were on a narrow road that had just been cleared. The view was impressive with the snow piled up on the sides, and the pine trees looked like the ones I had seen on Christmas cards.

While turning onto another small road, we realized that it had not been cleared by a snow plow yet. I got a little nervous, because the car made a different sound when passing over the snow. My husband looked at me and said that everything was fine, that he was driving slowly, and that he was following the tracks of the cars that had already passed. On the other side of the road, the snow was piled very high. The city we lived in was so small that nobody had come toward our home that morning.

After a few minutes, we saw some lights approaching from the opposite direction. To our concern, the car was driving in our lane. We drove slowly, giving it time to change course, and I heard my husband's voice saying aloud, "Go to your side," but the car did not move! He had to swerve to avoid being hit.

I do not remember screaming; I only saw the treetops incredibly close to my side, and in a second I felt the car land softly. There was no noise until I realized that we had left the road, and then my screams filled our car. The windows were completely covered, which prevented me from seeing where we were. My husband looked at me, took my hand, and said, "Nothing happened." With much effort, he opened the door on his side and walked around with great difficulty to help me open mine. Finally, after several attempts, he opened it and gave me his hand to help me out. At that moment, I went back to screaming.

We had practically flown in the air and dropped approximately thirty feet below the road. Around us were some pine trees, but we landed in a clearing. The snow that reached above my waist had cushioned the blow. I was wearing a coat over my dress, but I could feel that my legs were frozen.

We stood there without saying anything until we heard a distant voice coming from the road above. I could see a couple of people who were trying to signal to us, but we didn't understand what they were saying. More people came to gawk at our accident, and someone started shouting louder. My husband hugged me and explained, "They're asking us if we're okay!"

I do not know what expression was on my face, but surely it was one that showed total disbelief at that question. I asked my husband, "Why are they asking us that? Can they not see us?"

He looked up and then answered them: "Yes!"

The fear must have already passed, because now, crying, I said, "Do they not see us? Why did you tell them we're fine? I am not fine! Do you see where we are? We could have died! We are not fine!"

He hugged me tightly and said, "I told them we're fine because we're alive, and that's good!"

I do not know how much time passed while they helped us get out of there. I only know that after making sure we had no injuries, the police transported us home. During the day, some friends came to see us, always asking the same question as soon as we opened the door: "Are you okay?" I felt very tired. The last to visit us that afternoon was the couple that didn't change lanes. They brought us a delicious dinner, they apologized, they hugged us, and their last words before saying goodbye were, "We feel very grateful because you are okay!" I no longer had the strength to give my opinion about that statement.

It took a long time for me to really understand that question. *"Are you okay?"* No, I was not okay! To be okay, I needed none of this to have happened. It would have been nice if I had enjoyed a beautiful day, if they had brought me dinner when I could enjoy it and not when I felt so exhausted. But I remembered my husband's words: "…we're alive, and that's good!"

Whenever I hear or ask that question, I think sometimes we all want to say, *"Do you not see me? I'm not okay. It would be nice if I had better health, more money, or fewer challenges."* I try to always remember that day before answering!

When I wake up in the mornings, see myself in the mirror, and make sure I'm still breathing, the answer to the question "Are you okay?" appears in my mind and does not depend on how my own image looks. Yes. I am fine even when the challenges in my life are numerous or when the opposition seems never to disappear. I'm fine, even if my health is not the best or money is tight. I'm fine even when the problems come into my life like huge snowflakes trying to cover any path that leads me to reach an exit.

I'm okay because I still have the opportunity to find answers to my questions and solutions to my problems. Today, I'm fine because I can still enjoy mornings and magical days. I'm fine because I'm alive—the mirror confirms it.

4

CHANGE OF PLANS

Like many things in life, parent-teacher conferences at school seem to be held on days where our schedules are already packed full. Having four children, my husband and I decided to take turns during those days and take the opportunity to have a special outing with each child.

We'd received a paper with the available dates saying that I should call to make an appointment with two of the teachers. The paper was still attached to the refrigerator, because I had not yet decided on the ideal day and time. When returning from work that day, I asked my husband if he could go. He looked at the date in question and said yes, next week was perfect because he had no meetings in the evenings. I called the school and I felt grateful that there were still some spots available to meet with the teachers. Once I put a note in the calendar for the activities of the whole family, I could finally cross "scheduling parent-teacher conferences" off my to-do list.

During the next two days, our children talked about the things they would like to do with their father after visiting the school. They decided that they would go to their favorite ice cream place and then spend an hour at the park. Everything was planned.

I had also scheduled my three hours without the children to get ahead in some of my personal projects. I made a couple of calls to collaborate with a friend who was going to help me design an advertisement for a community event; I planned on spending fifteen minutes to go to her home and review the ad. Also, I made an appointment for a haircut.

The day of the meeting with the teachers arrived. I had prepared dinner early because thirty minutes after the children returned from school, they would eat dinner and get ready for their outing with their father. My youngest daughter, who was at my side 24/7, was freshly bathed and ready to go with them, too. When I was almost finished setting the table, the phone rang. I heard my son answer, and by his conversation I knew he was talking to his father. I grabbed the phone and heard him say, "I'm sorry, but I have a problem here, and I will arrive an hour late." I knew immediately that it really was something that was out of his control, because if he could, he would resolve any inconvenience to keep his word.

"Change of plans!" I told my children. "Get in the car and we will have dinner later." I hurriedly checked that my children had fastened their seat belts, and I handed them a fruit to eat on the way to the school. Surely the teachers would give me five minutes between one appointment and the other if I explained my predicament. I knew that if I was fast, I could be back the same time that my husband arrived home so that I would have the time to complete my errands.

I tried to keep my foot off the accelerator so as not to exceed the speed limit. I kept reminding myself that it was better not to face another setback in time that included the payment of a traffic infraction. As soon as I reached the parking lot, almost magically everyone was out of the van in a few seconds. If my son had not said, "Mommy, the principal always says that in school we shouldn't run," I would have done just that. But after listening to him and picking up my youngest, we settled on walking quickly.

Everything worked out perfectly. Twenty minutes later, we were back in the car, and I was happy to know that I would not miss my haircut appointment. I saw the clock, and I knew that everything would be fine. My children were very young and did not even sit in the front seat of the car yet. They knew that when Mommy drove, she could not talk; it was an established rule.

My five-year-old girl piped up: "Mommy, I need to talk to you." I told her that as soon as we got home we could talk. She explained that it was urgent, to which I again answered that she could wait a few minutes.

My son of almost twelve years, who understood the rule perfectly, told me, "Mommy, she has been thinking a lot for a good way to tell you this. She was going to tell Dad first, but we told her that telling you or Daddy is the same."

At that moment, looking in the rearview mirror, I saw their faces and I knew it was something important. "Okay, tell me what happened," I said as I tried to focus on the road again.

"Mom, someone kissed me!" And before I could say something else, she admitted, "And it was on the mouth!"

Looking at her again in the mirror, I realized how important it was for her to share that, so at the first opportunity I had, I stopped the car, turned it off, and put all my attention on her.

She explained how it happened and described her classmate in her kindergarten class. Finally, after all the details, she told me, "But don't worry, I did not like it!"

We returned home without hurry.

A minute after entering, the door of the house opened again and I heard my husband's voice. Possibly seeing the irritation on my face, he apologized for not having been able to arrive on time. He took my two-year-old girl from my arms and indicated that he would give our children dinner and continue with the plan we had set. I looked at the clock, which was next to a mirror on the wall, and I knew that if I ran again and put my foot on the accelerator, I could arrive at my appointments on time. I saw myself in the mirror, remembered my thoughts about the infraction, and smiled, knowing that my haircut would have to wait.

I canceled my appointments and decided to enjoy what had not changed: my family.

When I heard the laughter of my children talking to their dad about "the kiss," I realized that many times, the plans of life on our calendars are not always carried out. That does not mean that we are not committed to comply, but there are times when circumstances are "urgent," out of our hands, or when our conscience indicates that it is better to "change plans." The choice to be upset by changes, or to enjoy what has not changed, is our own very personal decision.

There are appointments that can be changed, plans that can wait, people who can excuse us—but there are moments that, if we let them pass by, will be lost to us forever.

5

DO NOT ABANDON ME!

My friend Anna and I were sitting on a bench in the park. That summer morning, the sky was a spectacular blue, but to be honest, I do not think Anna remembers it—when we are going through painful situations, we forget to appreciate nature. She had decided that this was the right place because she did not want anyone to see the evidence on her face from a night spent crying.

It was six o'clock in the morning when I received her call. Her words, almost intelligible, let me know it was time to leave the house and go meet her. During the time I took to get to her house, I only asked that she would not hurt herself, because I knew that she had done it before.

The door was open, and when I saw her, I knew she had had a very difficult night. She was sitting in an armchair, fully dressed and with her purse in hand, ready to go out. Her eyes were so swollen from crying that I doubted that she could even see, but she ran to me and asked me if we could go somewhere else, because being there reminded her of her desperation.

Anna had lost her only son in a car accident a couple of months before, and her husband had been with her at all times, but needed to return to work. Although for weeks he avoided going out of town, the night before he had to take a flight that would take him away from home for three days. It was devastating for my friend, and even though she cried, begged, and threatened, she could not get him to stop being responsible.

While sitting on the bench in the park, I hugged her and said, "It will only be three days!" She wiped away her tears, looked at me, and said, "You've never been through this; you do not understand. I feel like he's abandoning me!" I smiled, knowing that it was not true. The previous night, before he left, her husband wanted to be completely sure that we would be there for her. He explained that in addition to not having an option of staying, it was a good opportunity for him to reflect on his pain and pass though his grief without negatively affecting his wife.

"Anna, do you know why I have this scar on my left cheek?" I asked.

She tried to focus her eyes and said, "No, you've never told me."

"When I was little, one afternoon my parents decided to go somewhere without me, and they asked my grandmother to take care of me for a few hours. At four years old, I did not understand how they thought that was a good idea. I cried and shouted that they were abandoning me. When my parents walked away from my grandmother's house, they could still hear my screams. In my grandmother's one moment of carelessness, I opened the door and ran after them. Speed was greater than caution. I did not realize there was a concrete post, and my face hit it head-on. I should have felt great pain, because for a girl of my age, the injury must have been severe. Even though my parents had to return and spent a few hours with me in the hospital, I did not feel victorious in that moment. Some may believe that, in a way I achieved my purpose, but the price was very high, and I know it was not worth it.

"Anna, every time I look in the mirror and pay attention to the scar, I have absolute certainty that there are people in my life who love me and would never leave me. It does not matter how busy they are, if they are miles away from where I am, or if they are so close that I can hear them breathing. They are there every time I run after them, when

I feel lonely, sad, or simply need to share my anguish. They are the ones who feel pain when they see the scars that I have obtained through my life. I know they will take a moment to comfort me, even when with silent words I am shouting, '*DO NOT ABANDON ME!*'"

Many years have gone by since I received my scar. My friend has a scar of her own in her soul, but she knows that those who love her will never abandon her.

The fear of separation—the feeling that someone has left us behind when we are suffering, feeling unloved, or going through a complicated situation—can make us feel abandoned. Afflictions, insecurities, sorrows, and challenges are personal situations that we have to go through to gain experience and strength. But it is not necessary to face them alone; we can share them. Surely those moments of difficulty have marked our lives, reminding us that those who love us have not always avoided our sufferings, but have been there to sustain or lift us up. Even though many times we are alone, we need to remember that it does not mean we have been abandoned.

6

THE POWER OF A KISS!

After having children, you begin to realize how genes pass from one generation to another. Sometimes we feel grateful for what we inherit, and other times we ask ourselves, "Why me?" There are other things that become part of who we are that have nothing to do with genes. For example, there are certain home remedies we believe in and use faithfully because we have been told to do so, not because it has actually been tested and proven to work.

In my childhood and youth, my mother put a sizable number of remedies to the test. When my children started growing up, I was surprised to remember many of these remedies during situations where I could continue testing them. Most of the time, I believed they had worked for me, and I never imagined a day would arrive when I would doubt my mother's wisdom. But that day did come, and what I took from it changed my perception forever.

After many days of constant snow, I took my oldest son to the school bus and realized that it would be a sunny day. I wasn't the only one to notice the great weather; my two younger daughters did, too. When I got home from the bus stop, they both asked me if I would take them to the park. We looked out the window, and seeing the white blanket covering the ground from our home to the mountains, I showed them that it would be impossible to play there. The snow had stopped falling, but it was all clumped together a couple feet deep on the ground. Hoping that in a few hours the roads would be cleared, I promised Leah and DD that I would take them to their favorite fast food indoor playground.

Later, we found ourselves enjoying the beautiful, fresh scenery of fallen snow on our way to the restaurant. My two girls always kept me very busy, but knowing that I would have some quiet moments while they were having fun, I took my unfinished reading book with me. Surely, I would have time to read a little while we were at the restaurant.

While my daughters played, I became immersed in my reading. The twenty minutes that passed were glorious, right up until I heard Leah's cry. At four years old, she had so much energy that I had stopped counting the times she told me she was going down the slide. However, this last time she went down the slide, she came crying to me and showed me her little arm. The plastic from the slide had burned her arm with the friction.

Applying the knowledge I had inherited from my own mother, I hugged her, checked her arm, and on the very visible red burn mark, I gave her a kiss, telling her everything would be all right. I looked at the little grin on her face, which I imagine was just belief that a kiss would make everything better. I wiped her tears and told her to forget about the pain and go back to playing. Seeing her again at the top of the slide, I silently congratulated myself on my wisdom.

Later on, as I checked my watch, I realized it was time to go home. I told the girls it was time to put their shoes on to leave. Leah quickly came down and found hers. DD was still above in the playground, even after I asked her to come down. She broke into tears as I told her again it was time to go. And although I promised her we would be back soon enough, she still didn't mind me. After a few minutes, I asked Leah to take off her shoes again and go get her. When I realized that wasn't working either, and not knowing if it was against the rules of the place or not, I made the decision to go up and bring her down myself.

The place was designed for small children, so it wasn't that easy getting up to where my daughter sat. After much effort, I got to where DD was, and I thought I could get back down the same way I had come up. However, I immediately discarded that idea, because I would have to carry DD in my arms. I saw the slide and I knew it was my best option. DD, at two years old, thought it was fun to go down the slide with me, so she stopped crying. When we went down, one of my elbows rubbed against the plastic, and a few seconds later, I felt a great stinging pain.

When we were down the slide, I checked my elbow and saw that, just like Leah, I had burned my skin on the slide. My eldest daughter, when she heard me complaining, approached me, kissed my elbow, and said, "It's okay, it's okay, it's all better now!" I could not help but smile, but for some reason the painful sensation did not go away.

As I was driving, the sleeve of my coat was bothering my arm, so as soon as I got home, I checked it again. The red spot on my elbow was exactly the same as my daughter's, but I could not understand why it bothered me so much. That afternoon, I explained to my husband what had happened, and I complained once more about the small but persistent pain. At that moment, my daughter ran past us, and we asked her about her arm. She showed it to us quickly and disappeared, running again.

The next day, when I asked Leah if her arm still hurt, she said yes. "But I guess it doesn't hurt too bad, because you have not complained about it!" I remarked.

"Mommy, it does hurt a lot, but you gave me a kiss and you said it would all be better and the pain would go away," she replied.

I do not remember how long it took for my pain to disappear, but from that day on, I doubted if kisses truly cured scrapes or bruises in a magical way. I have the feeling that many times we minimize other people's pain in hard situations just because we only see the surface, and we hope that they will soon recover. Unfortunately, many times we are too busy to see what is underneath the surface.

No, I do not doubt that hugs and kisses help us to feel the love of those who give them to us when we go through any type of affliction. I hope we also understand that this does not instantly alleviate the suffering, but it will help give us hope that the moment will pass.

I want my children to inherit that knowledge and apply it and teach it to their own children one day, not because scientifically they have been proven to work, but from experience for generations they have been practiced. A kiss has a healing power that is hard to describe, but we all know that it works! Love doesn't make all of life's suffering go away, but love surely does help those hurtful moments become less painful.

7

I'M NOT LOOKING FOR ADVICE!

"You're the only one who understands me!" Raquel said between sobs. When I heard those words, I knew that she was going through one of those moments when we feel that life is unfair to one person, and that the worst thing is to discover that that person is us.

We had been sitting in the living room of my house for almost two hours. Raquel had come with the sole purpose of organizing a birthday party for her sister. She had asked for my help, and we took thirty minutes to finish fine-tuning every detail of what she had planned to do. Our conversation turned personal when I asked her how she could handle so many things at the same time and with such perfection. It was then that she explained to me, once again, what I already knew almost by heart: that she was not happy, or at least not in the way she had imagined it, and that her dreams were not becoming a reality.

"How is it possible that the years have gone by in such a way that without realizing it, they have turned me into what I am now?" I heard her question herself. I looked at her closely, and the only thing that went through my mind was, *"You are a beautiful, intelligent, and successful woman."* But that thought was to remain unsaid, because she did not want to hear about her good qualities or her good fortune. It was time to talk about her disenchantment, sadness, and especially about each of the situations that had trapped her in that state of unhappiness.

Raquel was a woman full of energy and great ideas. She had achieved great success in the professional field. Since our days in college, her perseverance and discipline were a part of her daily life. When I visited her at her home, she continued to prove to me that she would always be perfect in everything. I never saw anything out of place; the floors were bright, the bedrooms were immaculate, and the dinners were always exquisite. It reminded me of back in the day when everything in her backpack had its own place, and the notes in her notebooks were so organized. The rest of us ordinary mortals would borrow them to photocopy and be used almost as textbooks. But that was not enough to make her happy—at least, not at this moment.

"I've always tried to do my best at everything I've done," she continued. "I thought that was enough to make me happy. Look at me! Anyone would think that I have a perfect life, but they would never imagine what I have to go through."

When I heard her again, I realized that if she did not have the perfect life, it would be very difficult for someone else to obtain it. A couple of times during our conversation that day, she asked me, "What are you thinking about?" In trying to explain my point of view, she quickly interrupted me by stating the demonstration of weakness on her part and her knowing that my opinion was not very helpful, because the difficulties I faced in my life had almost no similarity to hers.

Finally, she told me, "Thank you very much for listening to me!" Yes, I had actually listened to her and tried to pay more attention to her feelings than to her words, knowing that that was the only way to show her that I understood her problems. In reality, though, most of the time I did not understand clearly what the problem was, because if a problem truly existed, the solution had not yet been found.

Counting all the real or imaginary challenges that a woman faces throughout her life sounds like an impossible mission. What I *can* say is that the only way we feel understood is when someone keeps their unsolicited advice to themselves, when we are heard as if we had the right to complain, when we can cry and show our disagreement over a period of time without being questioned, and when we are allowed to wipe away our tears before saying, "But I'm fine!"

Every time Raquel mentioned, "You are the only one who understands me!" I know that what she was really saying was, *"Thanks for not judging me, for not commenting, and especially for listening!"*

It is not always necessary to talk to show that you know or imagine what the person you love is going through. Nor is it essential to ask for details of these situations, because generally when one feels misunderstood, one cannot even explain the reasons. How do I know? Because many times, I've been Raquel. There are people who may think that my life is easy, that I do not have too many challenges, that the joys are many compared to the sorrows, and they are probably right. But there are times when the only thing I want the listener to understand is, "Please don't judge me. I'm not looking for advice. Just make me feel heard and understood!"

8

LOOKING FOR INSPIRATION

I have enjoyed many parties where I was only an attendee. In those instances, I am only expected to arrive on time, but I am not the one who organizes nor the one who is in charge; that's when I have the option to leave without having to wait until the end. Other times, I am the one who plans, gives assignments, and stays until the place is completely in order and hopefully better than when we arrived. I do not know which one is better. What I do know, is that I always try to enjoy any role I find myself in.

A group of friends and I decided to celebrate some birthdays together and, of course, enjoy a delicious dinner. On this occasion I was assigned to plan the party. Because experience has taught me that planning and taking action will prevent extra headaches, I asked some of my friends for help to make the party special for all those who attended. We chose the date, and we tried not to miss any details. The best thing about those moments we would share at the party is that we would have time to laugh and talk.

Finally the day arrived, and all of us who were going to help were there a couple of hours in advance. We wanted everything to be almost perfect. We put up the decorations and set the tables with red plates and matching napkins. The food was placed in trays on a table with a beautiful tablecloth; the desserts were arranged with great care on a green ladder that served as decoration. There were lights placed strategically to make the place feel cozy. The water was in a beautiful beverage dispenser, and soft music played in the background and would remain until we finished dinner.

When there were only five minutes left before our invited guests would arrive, I realized that something was missing: the cake. I asked one of my friends, and she, with great annoyance and frustration, let me know that whoever had said she would bring the cake was not here. Then she apologized to me, saying, "I was the one who suggested for her to bring a cake, and she said *yes*. I will make sure to tell her when I see her that she has ruined this party! How can we possibly celebrate birthdays without a cake?"

I suffered a moment of anguish. Then, like most people who find themselves in a bad situation, I got a moment of inspiration and said, "No one knows there was going to be a cake. We have many delicious desserts, and that will be enough."

Thirty minutes later, when the dinner was already being served, my friend who was in charge of bringing a cake walked in the door with nothing in her hands! It seemed strange that she did not arrive with her usual joy. As I approached her and embraced her, I felt prompted that I should not mention the cake and instead told her how happy I was to see her. I saw that her eyes were filled with gratitude, and I knew that it was because we did not make her feel guilty for what she had forgotten. I felt grateful because, although I was very busy, I had the opportunity to recognize that my only role was to help everyone enjoy the party.

We had a great celebration, the desserts were a great success, and no one noticed the absence of the cake. We all enjoyed each other's company and had a very special time. Gifts were opened and we sang.

When almost all of our guests had left, my friend took me by the arm and led me to the kitchen, where she began to cry. She told me that the party had been wonderful, but that she had hesitated to come because that morning she had been fired from work and did not know what she would do next. She was a single mom that supported her two children. She explained that during the party, someone mentioned that the company they worked for was hiring. My friend hugged me again and told me, "You realize that if I had not come to the party, I would still be crying at home."

We never mentioned the cake she had promised to bring. It was not necessary; the party had been a success anyway. At that moment, I was grateful to have followed the prompting to not scold her when she had arrived at the party empty-handed.

There can always be a celebration without cake.

Perfection is what we all look for when we are in charge of an event, and it is what we expect to reach when we set goals in our lives. Our responsibility is not only to plan, but also to look for inspiration and solutions in case setbacks occur. Many of the decisions to achieve success do not depend only on our disposition and abilities. We must show love, understanding, and compassion if someone fails to come through, and that includes ourselves. Remember that only a few know the plans to get everything right, and most won't notice if they are changed at the last minute. Excellence is not achieved when everything has gone almost perfectly, but when everyone involved has felt perfectly well.

9

RECOGNIZE IT!

Adolescence is the most difficult stage in life—not ours, to be specific, but our children's. Frequently, we strive to erase from our memories the difficulties we caused and the problems we found ourselves involved in. How many times did we think we were smarter than our parents? Possibly we were, once in a while, although at the time, they did not want to accept it either.

Since our youngest daughter, Shayla, was little, we discovered she disliked the rays of light in the dark sky or the thunder announcing a storm. She enjoyed the rain so much that she would run through it without any protection and jump in the puddles during the day, but as soon as there was a noise in the distance, we knew that if we were at home, we would find her in a closet or under the blankets, not in her bed, but mine or one of her older siblings'. If we were in the car, her face would be covered completely, and she would use her hands to block out the noise of thunder. Everywhere else, she sought refuge with us by hugging us in such a way that we could feel her shaking.

When this daughter was finally approaching adolescence, I knew that the time had come for her to leave some of her fears behind. As I did with her older siblings, I explained that we have to overcome the fears of our childhood because our understanding has developed in such a way that we can now see that many of those fears have no foundation. I explained to her that it was not easy for her siblings or me to accept her in our bedrooms, because it was silly that we had to be uncomfortable while her room was empty. She told me that she could not explain how she felt, just that she was afraid of those loud sounds and those bright flashes breaking the darkness of the night and that she hated not knowing what was about to happen. I explained to her that at home we should feel protected from the weather. She hugged me and told me that I was right, that she would no longer run to our beds. At that time, I thought I had solved the problem.

But the thunder and lightning made an appearance from time to time, so she decided to fulfill her promise and seek a new refuge: the basement. But she was not alone in her refuge, because a collection of stuffed toys that had accompanied her for several years found their way to the basement as well. Since it was not annoying anyone, we decided to let her spend those moments in an armchair that she had claimed as her property.

One Saturday morning, one of her sisters told me that Shayla was not in her room again. Knowing that it had rained heavily during the night, I remembered that I had experienced that same scene a few weeks ago, and that I thought the fear would disappear with time. When I went down the basement stairs to look for her, I realized that her place of refuge was empty. I called her name three times, and since she did not answer me, I searched for her more urgently. When I opened the door of our storage room, I found her sleeping peacefully on the floor on top of a pile of blankets with her dolls surrounding her and the light on. She opened her eyes and with a big smile asked, "Has it stopped raining? What time is it?" Since that room has no windows, she did not realize that it had already dawned a few hours ago.

During breakfast, my husband thought that since my methods did not work, it was his turn to talk to our daughter about the situation. Addressing her, he commented, "Sweetheart, you have a very beautiful bedroom that I would have been very happy with at your age. You have grown so much that you should stop being afraid not only of darkness, of thunder and lightning, but you should already sleep alone without all those dolls!" Our daughter, like every adolescent, had at her disposal the answer that supposedly we would never have announced at that age: "If you like my room so much, let's switch rooms. You say I am old enough to sleep alone and not be afraid, but I can't understand that at your age you do not think of sleeping somewhere else besides with my mom. I think you are the one who is more afraid!"

"But she is my wife!" exclaimed my husband.

"So what? She's my mom!" Finally, we all burst out laughing at this argument.

No matter how old we are, many of our fears may not have disappeared yet. We are probably frightened by not having someone at our side in the dark moments of life or when the storms lurk and bring with them problems that break the stillness of our days. It is difficult to accept that we do not always feel prepared to face certain challenges alone. Many times, we will only recognize that fact in the most difficult stages.

My daughter still has not overcome her fears, but she has discovered that her bedroom is the best place to face them. And as always, the storms will pass.

10

RISKING THEIR LIVES

I was born in a place where the only inspection that homes went through was when a father made sure the walls and the roof would protect his family from the wind, the sun, the rain, and the cold. I knew I could trust the place I called home. Not because the home was totally safe, but because the people who loved me and took care of me had my complete trust.

We came to live in a small town where—again—my parents were looking for stability for the family. The tiny house is only a vague memory in my mind. Although I close my eyes to try to focus on the place, I cannot grasp all of the details. I think it was on a corner and that it was gray. I do not know what the dimensions of the only room I had were, but I do remember that the ceiling was made of sheets of asbestos.

I have many memories of my childhood, but there are things that did not matter so much, and I allowed time to erase them. On occasion, I turned to my family to collect pieces for the puzzle of memories. For the purpose of this story, I want to keep the memories I have of that place focused on the great lesson I learned there.

The rain was a frequent visitor in that town. At night, the sound of the water against the sheets of asbestos was soothing to me. In the mornings, when leaving home, I enjoyed the smell of grass and the wet earth so much that sometimes I wanted to put a bit of mud in my mouth. The best of times was when the rain continued during the day, and I ran to and fro, trying to drink the water that fell from the sky.

There was one night when the rain stopped being fun. The lightning and thunder became too frequent, and the wind made such a strange noise that the laughter disappeared. We all started to feel a little afraid to see that the roof of the house seemed to rise and then fall back into place. We thought that the storm would pass quickly just like other days and that in a few minutes we would be asleep. However, it was not so.

When the water entered the house and the wind blew even harder, my parents told us children to get under the only table we had. Seven children are too many to fit under a small table, but we followed their instructions. I remember seeing my dad on one side of the room hanging from the heavy sheets, trying to get the wind not to take them; on the other side, my mom did the same. The storm continued to rage, and I am positive I closed my eyes. I hope I was brave and did not cry.

Once again in my mind, I see my parents protecting themselves by taking cover under a thin mattress. I believe that they knew that if one of the asbestos sheets were to fall down, it would hurt them because of how heavy each sheet was. During those minutes that seemed like an eternity to me, I imagined my parents trying to save a ship in the middle of the storm. My imagination makes me remember them with anguish reflected on their faces in the illumination of the lightning and the water running down their faces. Those are the memories that I want to save from that place, because that is where I learned that my parents were willing to risk their lives to protect us.

Maybe we slept in wet blankets that night after the storm passed, but I can assure you that the next morning, my father inspected the roof again. Since he did not know if we would need to survive a new storm that night, he tied the asbestos sheets that were misplaced by the storm until he was sure that everything was fine, and then he went to work. The new day certainly brought calm feelings, since I remember jumping in the big puddles of water around the house, having fun and getting wet.

In that tiny home on the corner, I learned that love without conditions exists. No matter the location of the house where we live or how it is built, there will always be storms in our lives that will make us feel anguish. I learned that if we fight against those moments that try to destroy our happiness, we can survive—even in the most adverse circumstances— if we seek protection. I realized that it is true that storms happen, and that we should smile when tranquility appears again in our lives, but most importantly, we should make sure we are prepared in case these storms return.

11

SHE DOESN'T KNOW!

I t had been three years since we moved to the house we are living in now. Changes were beginning to be noticed, not only because the trees that had been planted years ago were starting to give our yard a different look, but also because the people in our family grew from three to five.

The day looked sunny, and I felt inspired to work in the garden. The flowers were beautiful, but I knew they would look better when we removed the weeds around them. That morning I walked outside, determined to finish the dreaded task. I grabbed the youngest of my daughters and placed her on a small swing near the porch, where there was a small roof that would protect her from the sun. My two oldest children brought out some of their toys, ready to entertain themselves while I got to work.

The yellow flowers we had planted a couple of years before were incredibly beautiful and made me feel happy just by looking at them. Neither my husband nor I had much knowledge about gardening, but we knew we had made a good decision by following the advice of our neighbors to buy flowers that bloomed even after the heavy snowfalls that fell during the winter.

The cleaning task was not easy, but as time went by and I realized I was halfway done, it was enough to push me to continue.

Seeing that the children were entertained, I quickly entered the house for a drink of water, because the temperature was rising. As I brought each of my children a glass of water and helped the youngest one drink hers, I noticed that two yellow flowers had been pulled out. I asked the children what had happened, and my oldest told me that they wanted to help me. He had brought some of the weeds to the trash and the youngest also wanted to do the same thing as Mommy.

"We do not pull flowers out," I said softly as I saw some of the yellow petals between her hands. The baby repeated the word "no," and we all laughed. I continued with my chore while my son took care of removing the remains of the flowers his younger sister had pulled out.

A few minutes later, I caught a glimpse of my daughter, who now had a few flowers clenched in her little hands! Now my tone of voice was firmer when I said, "You cannot pull out the flowers!" As I took the flowers from her hands, I began to feel like giving up on my project. Still, the morning was beautiful, so I went on with my task of pulling weeds.

The moment ceased to be pleasant when I discovered once again that my daughter was going to the garbage bag and depositing more flowers in it. "I told you that you should not pluck the flowers!" This time my voice had more than a hint of frustration, and my little girl began to cry.

My son, who had been watching us, said in all his wisdom, "Mommy, I think she doesn't know that these are called flowers." He took his sister by the hand with great affection and calmly said, "This is a flower," and to make her understand better and having learned to spell, he repeated it. "F-l-o-w-e-r, flower. Flowers don't get plucked because they are pretty and Mommy likes them." He hugged her and invited her to help him pick the weeds that were still on the ground and throw them in the trash.

That was a very special morning to me. My daughter learned not to pluck the flowers because someone had the sensitivity to teach her something that seemed so obvious to me but not to her.

Sometimes in our lives we take for granted what others understand, imagine, or know is right. Just because there are things that are obvious to us, we think they do not need an explanation. We should not believe that someone has knowledge in a certain area without asking. Many misunderstandings and dislikes could be avoided if we ask, take time, and explain what is not yet known.

12

SILENCE

Silence is what every mom lacks from the moment she receives the baby that she has waited so long for. There is no way to explain why losing a moment of quietness is no longer important to her. For a mom, even if she does not get enough sleep or forgets that she exists, the only thing that is important is the little person who can now sleep in her arms.

I arrived... and I broke the silence that my mother had enjoyed for a very brief period of time. My older brother was about to turn three years old, and I am sure that he loved me from the moment he first saw me, just like my parents—although like every male, he must have felt a little disappointed to know that the new baby was only a girl.

When I opened my eyes for the first time, I imagine I saw my mother's face and thought it was a blessing that someone so beautiful could exist. I probably felt the strong arms of my father hugging me gently. From that moment on, I am sure I felt that both of my parents were not only willing to give their lives for me, but to make my life meaningful. I depended on them completely, but even when babies cannot talk or take care of themselves in any way, I have the feeling that babies can think, give thanks, and enjoy the love and affection they receive from those who love them and those that they will love for the rest of their lives.

And that's me, the one who thinks, gives thanks, and loves not only those who were there for the first dawn of my life, but all those who have come to me during the subsequent years and even those who will be part of my future.

Yes, on many occasions we can long for silence in our lives, but I have learned that this silence should not only serve to disconnect us from the sounds and voices around us, but to ponder quietly on what we have enjoyed, what we have laughed at, and even what we have cried about in our journey through this life.

Thinking is a privilege that we all possess, and for this we need silence. But as incredible as it sounds, and even when no one utters a word or produces sounds around us, thinking can make that silence end. The mind begins to hear voices and pays attention to all the sounds that have been part of your life and are stored in a file that can be opened frequently. The hope is that we can remember those moments that help us feel grateful for the opportunity we have to be on this earth. Those moments that break the silence.

13

THE COLD WILL DISAPPEAR

Even though the air was no longer frigid when I left the doctor's office that morning, I was shaking. As I let my body fall into the passenger seat, I felt sick and heavier than ever. When my husband took me by the hand, I could no longer contain the tears, and then, like many women in the same situation, I asked out loud, "Why? Why me again?"

When I said goodbye to my children earlier that day to attend my monthly appointment, they kissed me on the stomach and said goodbye not only to me, but to the baby we had been waiting for so long. A couple months before, we had confirmed to the children that no, I was not getting fat, but in a little more than four months we would have a baby. Everyone was happy, especially our only son, who assured us that this was a little brother; that after three girls, he would have someone to share his room with. The plans began, and even though our youngest daughter was almost two years old, she already seemed to understand that soon there would be someone smaller than her at home.

We had been careful not to share the news with our children until we felt that everything was safe. We had previously gone through a situation that had caused us a lot of pain, and we wanted to prevent that from happening again. Five months were enough, though, because that morning they would give us the appointment to go to the hospital in a couple of weeks. There we would know if our son would finally have someone to share his toys with.

When we arrived at the doctor's office, we were greeted by a nurse we had just met and who was very kind. She told us that the doctor would be with us in a moment. During my previous pregnancy, the doctor realized when talking with my husband that they had acquaintances in common, and that always made the visits more pleasant. The doctor arrived and began chatting with us. When he pulled out the device to listen to the baby's heartbeat, I felt the same quiet happiness as always. I closed my eyes to enjoy that moment.

Silence. I opened my eyes just as the doctor stood up, saying that he probably needed to change the batteries of the device. My heart froze, and the cold gel that had been put on me spread a chill throughout my body. I did not need him to confirm what I knew was happening.

When the door opened again, I felt as if the snow that had accumulated from the previous days had entered the small room. My husband took my hand and hugged me tightly as the doctor confirmed that the baby's heart was not beating anymore. I do not remember what happened between that moment and when I was in the car.

After several minutes in the parking lot, unable to speak, we headed home. We didn't think about what we would say to the children or what would happen in the days to come. We were just trying to let each other know that everything would be fine. We were not looking for the nonexistent answer to my question of *"Why?"*

When I got home, it was the usual party. The children bounced around happily. It was then that I realized an important truth: I should be crying over the happiness I felt when I saw four little ones running around, trying to tell me the adventures they had with the girl who had taken care of them for a couple of hours. The cold began to disappear.

I had to go visit a family that afternoon, and even though I wanted to go to bed and cry, I decided that it was best to continue with what was planned for that day. A small cake rested on the table, waiting to be delivered, and I took it on my way out the door. As I got in the car, I glanced in the mirror to make sure that the marks of my pain could not be seen; I was going to a home to help, not to receive consolation.

When I arrived at the house of this family, the minutes passed quickly. They explained to me how difficult it was for them to have to battle with the problems of one of their children and also mentioned that the father had lost his job. Seeing the cake that I had baked with my children that morning, the mom of that family said, "Let's forget for a moment our problems and celebrate that we are fine—or are cakes not meant to celebrate with?" We all laughed.

When I returned home, I knew that I should not procrastinate explaining to the children what was happening, so together with my husband we explained the situation in the sweetest way we could. Everyone seemed to understand naturally what I could not come to terms with. When I could not control my tears, my eleven-year-old son hugged me and said, "Mommy, what I like is that you're fine."

I would like to say that I didn't cry anymore, but I did. I cried many times, and even now when I remember it, I feel a bit emotional. The sensation of loss will never be forgotten. I learned that we are going to cry until the moment that we can smile again; this is why "we need to look for a reason to celebrate!"

I still have no answer to the question "Why me?" What is clear for me is that facing a situation like this has given me the opportunity to better understand those who are suffering this kind of pain. I know that the words "everything happens for a reason" have no meaning at the moment of feeling lonely, sad, or heartbroken. It does not help to hear that our sadness will soon disappear, because the pain is now, and nothing and no one will replace the desire to have those babies in our arms.

I also know that the cold we feel when we are discouraged, sad, disheartened, or in pain only disappears when someone clothes us with love and understanding and shares the burden of our sorrow. We don't have to lie, hide, suffer, or silence our pain. Knowing that adversity will always be present in our lives, we need to focus more on everything we have instead of everything we don't have.

14

THE FIRST STEP

It is not easy to admit to a group of children that age does not always make you the one with the most knowledge. I learned that lesson when I had the opportunity to tend some of my nieces and nephews one afternoon while my brother and his wife attended a work party.

It was almost Christmas, so the chances of having the children play outside were low because of the cold weather and the fact that the sun went down so early. By unanimous decision (not counting my vote, of course), everyone voted to watch a movie and designated me as the popcorn maker. With only two boys in a group of nine, there was no possibility of choosing something other than a princess movie. My son, Oliver, and his cousin, Erik, were not interested in watching this kind of movie, so they chose to play with their cars in a corner of the room while the girls swooned over the handsome prince rescuing the princess.

After the movie ended, the children agreed that it was time to have dinner. While the children and I sat around the table waiting for the pizza to bake in the oven, we began talking about princess movies, especially the one that we had just watched. The boys said that those kinds of movies were so boring because all the princesses were the same except for their hair color. The girls disagreed and began to explain that even though there were a few similarities between the princesses, everyone was unique. Even the youngest of the girls, at only four years old, knew that the princesses were not the same, because each one had a different background story.

I asked the girls if they considered themselves princesses. With eyes full of disbelief that I could doubt, all the girls answered in unison, "YES!"

One of the boys let out a loud laugh and said, "But sometimes you are little witches!" We all continued to laugh as the girls denied that statement.

I asked them who their favorite characters were, and each girl identified with someone. However, the girls could not understand why the princes were not favorites for the boys. They explained to the girls that they would rather be a superhero.

Continuing my questioning, I asked them what they thought of the character that was a stepmother. I was surprised that none of the children had an opinion about her. So I asked the children, "Do you know what a stepmother is?" With great confidence, Emma, the oldest of the children, replied, "A stepmother is a mom who takes many, many steps!"

I smiled at her response and asked her to explain her answer. She said, with all the wisdom she had gained at the age of nine, "The stepmother is someone who takes many steps to be the mom of someone who is not her child. The first step is to fall for the child's daddy. The second step is to love and understand the child, sometimes that's not easy, so that's why she gets angry. But at least she tries."

Her sweet and innocent response amazed me so much that I walked around the table, hugged my beautiful niece, and told her that today she had taught me something important. She then whispered in my ear, "Auntie, when you need to know something, you can always ask me."

That day, I learned that even if we have lived longer, read more, or consider ourselves wiser, there is always someone who can, with simplicity, teach us the unwritten meaning of a word. It is special to know that there are people on this earth that have a simple and clear vision on life and seek to see the positive side of any situation.

There is no doubt that the first step to achieve what we want is to simply take steps toward who we want to become. It will not always be easy, and sometimes we will be filled with frustration, but the path will always exist. Our goal should be to move our feet toward the path that will help us achieve our dreams.

15

THE GIFT OF COMMUNICATION

Although our first son never demanded to have everything he wanted, he knew that being the only child for almost four years gave him certain advantages. After he turned two years old, he always asked for a few minutes to go to the toy section in the store; "I just want to look" was his request. He did not always come out with something new, but he told us what he would like to have, "...when we could buy it for him."

This time it was different. Upon entering the store, he said, "Mommy, I need to buy something for my church teacher because tomorrow is Valentine's Day, and I want to take something to her." His teacher always made sure that he felt good in class, which made him feel admiration and lots of love for her. When I heard his words, I was moved, because I understood that in developing love for other people, my son was forgetting a little about himself. We spent some beautiful moments finding the perfect gift. He handled it carefully, and he took care of it during the whole trip home. We enjoyed wrapping the present, and I helped him write a little card where he drew a picture.

That night, before going to bed, my son carefully placed the card on the gift and then set it right next to his bed; he wanted to be sure that nothing would happen to the gift during the night. The next morning when he woke up, it was the first thing he saw. He took care of it and played so much with it that the wrapping paper began to show some wear. When he was ready to leave for church, he once again checked the package and held it in his hands with great care after buckling his seat belt. At last, the moment came when he said goodbye to me and ran to where he would deliver his surprise.

A couple of hours passed before I saw him again. His little face was full of sadness, with as many lines as the wrapping paper around the little box he held in his hands. He said, "She didn't want it, Mommy! She did not like it!" I felt very confused and very hurt to see him so affected. I took the gift, hugged him tightly, and tried to think of an explanation. I could not come up with one, and since I also needed an answer, I took my son by the hand and returned inside to find out why his teacher didn't accept his gift.

Everything had been a mistake on both sides. He gave his teacher the gift without saying a word. She thought he just wanted her to take care of it, so at the end of class she returned it to him. The teacher felt so afflicted after hearing about the misunderstanding she turned quickly to my son and embraced him, telling him how grateful she was for him thinking about her and hoping he would forgive her for not understanding. My son's face, once filled with sorrow, lit up, and that pair of dimples I love so much appeared again on his cheeks. It was the magic of acceptance that made him feel joy. After the embrace, he began to run as fast as his two little legs could go, showing me that he was happy again.

How much confusion can exist between two people who love each other if we assume that the other person knows what we are thinking? How much pain does it cause to receive rejection after a display of affection? If we are careful to avoid filling our hearts with resentment for something we don't understand, if we seek the true answer to our doubts, we will find that those who have really shown love cannot stop doing it from one moment to the next. When we have clarified any thought or action that has brought us pain, feelings of peace and tranquility will return. Love does not change without a reason, but many times it is necessary to open the gift of communication.

16

THE RIGHT FOCUS

The afternoons after returning home from school were always wonderful. The hours seemed to pass slowly, giving us many moments to enjoy. Together with my brothers, I found there was not much time to get bored. Not only did we have the opportunity to climb trees, play with friends, or watch television, there was also time to do homework, read, and help at home.

We had moved to a small ranch owned by a friend of my father. During those years, my younger brother increased his collection of costumes, so it was not strange to see him with a blue, white, or yellow mask to represent a wrestler or the famous black mask of the Lone Ranger.

It seemed strange to me that one day, when we got off the bus, my brother did not run to put on the boots that our parents had recently bought for him. The only reason my brother did not wear the boots 24/7 was because they were not part of the school uniform. He would even wear the boots to bed!

That afternoon, my father returned home early with his camera in hand, and when he saw us all together in the yard, he said he wanted to take a picture of us. Oddly enough, even though my dad was a photographer, we rarely had the opportunity to pose for his camera.

While telling us to settle down and get in a position where there was good lighting, my father noticed that the boots he had bought a few days ago for my brother were not being used. When he asked my brother about the boots, my brother answered that he did not want to use them that day. Without giving any further explanation, he settled down in his place so that the photograph could be taken.

My dad looked at him and said, "Go put on those boots, because I want them to be seen. Plus, the boots suit you very well." My brother ran to the house, and we sat down by a fence to wait for him.

After several minutes, my brother returned without the boots. We knew something was wrong. He told my dad that he could not find them, and his eyes began to fill with tears. My brothers thought our younger brother was crying because my dad looked very angry, but to this day, I think that he cried out of fear that he had lost one of his most precious treasures.

My father sent us all to look for the boots, so we ran to look everywhere they could possibly be. After several minutes of tears, screaming, and anger, another one of my brothers found the boots! Happily, my brother took off the shoes he was wearing and threw them aside to put on his boots. Now he was ready to be in the photograph.

Finally, once we were all posed and smiling, my dad counted, "One, two, three!" and we heard the click of the camera. At that moment, we all forgot the moments of anguish lived minutes before. My dad reminded my brother that he should learn to put his boots where he would remember them and as soon as my dad disappeared from our sight, we returned to our games until it was time to go inside.

No one mentioned the search for the boots again until a week later. The picture was on the table, and my mom talked about how much we had grown and how good we looked. When my older brother saw the photograph, his laughter took us by surprise, but then we all gathered around the table and looked at it. We laughed so much that our stomachs ached and our eyes filled with tears. My mom did not understand why we were laughing, so we explained the story of the lost boots, and then she joined our laughter.

The portrait spoke for itself: three boys with smiling faces and one girl with hair out of place but with a big smile, too. Behind the children, you could see the tree that we had climbed many times and a fence that divided our house from the fields of alfalfa. The clothes we wore showed the colors of joy that characterized us during those days … but what about the boots? Well, my dad simply focused on the good and captured the joy on our faces, but forgot to include our feet! The boots did not appear in the picture, because in the end, they were not that important!

Every time we remember that experience, we agree that in our lives we often concentrate on things or situations that make us suffer, cry, or feel anger or frustration. But after those often unavoidable times, we must focus on the most important thing: our happiness. I do not remember the color or the size of the boots, but I still remember the happiness of those years, and for me, that is focusing on the right side of life.

17

THE VALUE OF WHAT YOU OBTAIN AND OF WHAT YOU RECEIVE

When seeing the mountain of gifts that our first and only son had received on his third birthday, we, as parents, were filled with gratitude. We thought that those toys and clothes could last him for the next five years if he did not grow up. As the days passed, we realized that each toy lost its charm quickly, and our son, knowing that there were toys in the sealed boxes, would ask to open one more. At some point, there would be no new toys to open. We were afraid that our son could possibly demand to go to the store and buy even newer toys.

My husband and I both had humble beginnings. We had grown up sharing what little we had with all of our siblings. Although it was hard at times, it made us appreciate everything we owned. My husband and I talked about the situation our son was getting into. We doubted that a young child could understand our concerns, but we sat down and explained to him what we had experienced at his age. We explained that these toys were too much for a single child and yes, they were his, so he should be grateful, take care of them, and enjoy them more.

He asked us if there were still children around the world that are growing up the same way we did. We told him yes, there were, and then he asked us to look for a child that he could share his toys with. We found a couple of families where the toys were more than welcome. To our surprise, our son had decided to give away not only some of toys that had already been opened but also those he had not used yet, which brought us greater joy.

Near his fourth birthday, we had moved to another part of the country. We did not know many people, so we decided to take our son to a toy store for fun. While strolling through the store aisles, his interest centered on a toy motorcycle. He hopped on it and said, "I want this." Again, we worried. After the mountain of toys the year before and the toy motorcycle this year, what would he expect for his next birthday?

We let him continue admiring what he wanted, and then we explained that it was very expensive, but if he worked and saved he could have it. His eyes lit up when we discussed some ideas of how to earn money. Over the next few weeks, we baked cookies that he sold to neighbors or to his dad's co-workers. He also did extra chores around the house, and we paid him for those. In those few weeks, we watched as his jar of coins almost filled up.

On his birthday, he woke up knowing that after much effort, he could finally buy his toy motorcycle. He put all his money in a bag and we headed to the store. When we arrived, my husband went ahead of us to explain the situation to the cashier. He wrote a check and asked her to accept the bag of coins my son would give her, and then later we would return for the bag of coins without my son noticing.

Carrying his heavy backpack filled with coins and rolled-up dollar bills, our son examined the toy motorcycle. He touched it and proudly said to the girl at the counter, "I want to buy this motorcycle." The girl told him the price and with great satisfaction, our son took out all the money he had and asked, "Here's the money. Can I take the toy now?"

From that day on, all of my son's attention went towards that toy motorcycle. Every day he would clean it, after a ride he would put it back safely where it belonged, and he would make sure to recharge the battery so that it was always ready for him to ride. Even though he was always careful with all his belongings, there was a big difference between his appreciation for what he had struggled to obtain and what he had received as a gift. The day he discovered that he was too big for his beloved toy motorcycle, he was ready to give it to someone else, but not before being sure that it was in tip-top condition.

This was a great lesson that we have tried to teach our daughters and do our best to remember as adults in our daily lives. We shouldn't just simply appreciate and take care of something more when we have earned it; we should also be grateful when we receive something as a gift. A gift is a way someone can show their love towards us, because they are willing to share what they have obtained with effort.

We must always be happy for opportunities to prove to ourselves that we can pay the price of what we want, although there will undoubtedly be many times someone will give us their help without us noticing it. Above all, we must take care of our possessions, because whether new or used, there will always be someone with whom we can share them.

18

TRANSLATION, PLEASE!

One summer afternoon, my daughters and I decided to go to a Women's Fair. We were very excited because we knew that all of us would find something that we would like. The year before we had a fabulous time at the event, and this year would be no different. As we arrived at the fair, we worried because the parking lot was full, and we thought we would not be able to get a spot quick enough to start our shopping. As discouragement started settling in, we looked over and saw a car exiting. We could not believe it! It was going to be our lucky day.

As soon as we walked through the doors, we heard the buzz of many women talking around us while visiting the different booths that were set up. My girls and I excitingly started to list the different things we wanted to look for. Then, all of a sudden, a booth for hair products caught my attention. It was a brand that I was familiar with because my sister-in-law always used it. I walked closer, and the woman began to tell me the benefits of using the products. After having a conversation with her in English, exchanging questions and answers, I decided that I wouldn't buy anything that she was selling because I could see that it was expensive.

While I was thanking her for her time, my daughter DD told me in

Spanish that she was going to look at the things ahead. The saleswoman turned her attention towards my daughter and asked her if she could translate the things she was explaining to me. For a moment DD looked at her confused, but as realization settled in, she faced the lady with a big smile and replied, "My mom speaks English!" The woman looked at me and said, "Oh!" and then continued her conversation trying to sell me the product.

In that moment, I laughed and I told my daughter in English, "Please tell her thank you for the information, but maybe we will come back later." My daughter, going along with it, started to repeat my words.

The lady laughed and said, "I understand what your mom is saying."

Smiling, I said, "I am surprised that after ten minutes of having a conversation with me, you realized that we don't need someone to translate for us." She apologized, and I bought a shampoo from her.

How many times has it happened that after talking to someone in the same language, we feel they don't understand us? Possibly, we have exchanged advice, experiences, feelings, or ideas with our spouse, children, family, or friends. We then ask somebody to explain to them what we are trying to say, even though we are the ones who haven't paid attention to their words.

True communication doesn't just include talking and listening in the same language; it is the acceptance that we don't all have the same point of view. There is a high possibility that we are the one who needs the translation after we get an answer that we neither want to hear nor expect. Hopefully, someone helps us understand that our perspective isn't always the most accurate or perfect. Perhaps when this happens, and we apologize for our lack of understanding, the other person is willing to accept that what we said was with a purpose to help and not only to obtain what we wanted.

19

TWO POINTS OF VIEW

U sually, I did not venture into the store by myself with three small children. I always tried to go when my husband could go with me or when he stayed at home with the children. That day I had no choice. My husband was out of town for a few days, I had to go shopping, and I hoped that everything would be fine.

When we were young children, the only thing that most of us wanted to do was run, shout, and play. Knowing that, I explained to my young children that I expected them to behave themselves, that there were more people around, and that we would be there for just a brief moment.

I placed the two little ones in the shopping cart, and I asked my oldest son to walk by my side. For three seconds everything seemed to work perfectly until I had to stop for a moment and open one of the refrigerators to grab a gallon of milk. As it often happened, my son took a toy away from his sister without warning. She screamed, trying to recover the toy—she had not been playing with it, but now that it lay in other hands, it was of almost incalculable value. Hearing her older sister whimper, the youngest also cried.

Wanting to recover peace, I asked my son to return what was not his. In an ideal situation, he would deliver the toy so there would be no more complaints, and the crying would end. In reality, he refused, and I had to tear the toy out of his hands, which resulted in him crying also. At that moment, I knew that if we had not been in a public place, I would have joined them in their complaints, and we would all have started to shed tears.

Unexpectedly, a woman approached me and spoke to the children with a sweet voice. While looking into my eyes, she told me that I should be very happy to have such beautiful children; she always thought that the cry of children was a special way of saying, *"Here I am."* She also thought that mothers should respond by thinking, *"Yes, despite these circumstances, it is a blessing and a miracle that you are here with me!"*

Her comments were accurate, because even when the children did not stop crying, made me feel better. She went on her way, and I kept looking for the items I needed.

When it was time to pay, the discontent started again, but I was not worried because I knew we would be leaving soon. As I fit the bags of groceries into the cart, I heard the voice of someone saying that they did not know how it was possible for someone to be so inconsiderate in bringing such rude children to the store where their moans annoyed everyone who heard them.

I slowly turned my head and realized that they were, of course, talking about me, and the woman expressing her opinion was very similar to the one that had shared some wisdom with me a few moments before! I laughed, because such a comparison was absurd. Yes, both were women and almost of the same age, but in no way did they resemble each other. What made them totally different was not their dress or the color of their hair, but in their attitude towards life.

On my way back home, I saw my three sleeping children through the rearview mirror, and a tear welled up when I recognized that they a blessing and a miracle in my life. I remembered the two women, and for one I felt admiration. I hoped that she would have a full life of happiness where the solutions to the challenges were found in a more pleasant way. Then the image of the other woman came to mind, and I felt sad because I knew that she was dissatisfied not only with that moment, but with life itself. They were two women with two different points of view.

This image has endured with me. Undoubtedly, the way we react in critical moments is the way we will be remembered, whether we are directly involved or only spectators. Our actions can indicate to us what state of happiness we are in or how far we are from reaching it. Hopefully, we are counted among those who awaken admiration among those who constantly tread the space of happiness and teach others how to get there.

20

WITH THE SAME SHOES

W hen I was a young girl, going to my dance classes was one of my favorite hobbies. I loved the challenge of learning new choreographies and above all, dance gave me the opportunity to meet new people and see new places. We had practice three times a week, and because the people in my dance class saw each other so often, we felt like a big family and that we had known each other all our lives! Of course, for some people, fourteen years doesn't seem that long, but for us, that was all the years we had lived.

After class, a few of us would stay afterwards to practice choreography steps we had forgotten or practice dance routines we would get lost in. Since we didn't want to mess up in our dances, my teammates and I knew that repeatedly practicing would allow us to never go through that embarrassment during our actual performance. Besides staying after to practice, we would talk about the things we were going through and in return, we learned about the latest events in the wider teenage world.

Not everyone in our class had the income to buy new dance shoes or the required costumes. Years before, our dance teacher had the idea of doing fundraising events that would give us the money necessary to buy shoes or help with payment of the costumes. Everything that we received was collected and spent wisely. Our responsibility was to take care of the items we used and return them in the best condition possible, because we never knew when we or someone else would wear them again.

We all had a pair of black dancing shoes, which we used most often and practiced with. We learned how important it was to practice with those special black shoes, because no one liked the idea of sore feet after a performance. Almost none of us invested in white dancing shoes, so they were only occasionally used, and even when we had to learn all the choreography that required them, only a few of us were chosen to perform in those dance numbers. Those were the shoes that were bought with the collected money.

I had taken someone's place when they were not able to come to the practices, but it was only temporary. I had never danced during an actual performance. Not having a pair of white shoes was never a concern for me until after almost two weeks of practice. We learned that one of our team members would not perform because she had moved out of town, and my teacher announced that I would take her place permanently. When I went to the studio closet to look for a pair of shoes, I realized that they were all smaller than my shoe size, and when I tried to fit into them, I felt pressure and pain in my feet. Three of my friends had the same size shoe as me, but two of them had bought their own shoes, and the other had been using hers for a few months to perform in.

Realizing my situation, my friend Karina told me that very soon she would need some bigger shoes, so I could use hers. She was an only child and always mentioned how lucky I was to have so many brothers. I said that it was possibly much better not to have to share everything that was in the house. Even though I made that comment, I felt that my brothers were very valuable to me. I would never trade them for clothes or shoes ... well, maybe sometimes!

I wore my regular black dance shoes during the remaining practices. Karina's mother told me not to worry, and reiterated that I could use her daughter's white shoes because they were going to buy some new ones in her size. When the day arrived, I felt very happy not only to see my friend's new shoes, but to also know I would be able to wear her old ones in the performance. When we arrived at the place and changed, I was grateful again for having the appropriate-colored shoes. I put them on, and although I felt them slightly tight on one side of my foot, I knew they would be fine.

When I returned after the first two dance numbers, however, I knew that I could not continue with them, because they were painful enough that I wanted to cry. Another one of my friends offered to exchange her shoes for the ones I was currently wearing. I thanked her, but when I tried them on, I realized that although they were the same size, my foot did not fit because hers were very thin. Karina then suggested that I could wear her new shoes, but they were bigger than my size, and we knew that wearing them could also create a problem. My last option was to change shoes with Monica who took hers off and did not hesitate to help me. I danced with her shoes for two more numbers, and they did not actually injure my feet, but they created pain in my heel.

When I finally had the opportunity to wear my own black shoes in the other dances, I felt so happy that I forgot the pain in my injured feet. The next week I felt determined to practice with the shoes that my friend had kindly given me, so I put alcohol inside the shoes and wore thick socks when practicing to help stretch them out. As the weeks passed by, I noticed that the white shoes were getting as comfortable as the black ones I owned. Not only were they my size, but my feet had grown accustomed to the shoes and molded them to my comfort.

Some years later, when someone mentioned that we should not judge someone else unless we have walked in their shoes, I could not relate to that phrase because I remembered my sore feet at fourteen years old. My friends and I not only walked but danced with the same shoes. For them they were comfortable, but not for me. My dance teammates did not understand how the shoes could hurt me and not them if we wore the same shoe size. And I didn't understand how the shoes were comfortable for them.

We used the same shoes, but our experiences while wearing them were not the same. No, we cannot judge. I used someone else's shoes, and although they were my size, they left my feet sore until I molded them to what felt comfortable to my own feet.

Can we truly say that we know what someone else feels when we have worn the same shoes? Although my friends and I had the same shoe size, our feet were shaped completely different. Maybe our arches, toes, or even our way of treading were not the same.

The solution to a problem is not the same for everyone. For some, the solution can be easy to find, for others it can be difficult, and there will be those who think that the problem is impossible to solve. What is certain is that each one of us takes a different amount of time to mold certain circumstances in our lives, until, as with shoes, we learn how to walk or dance with them.

It is the same with the life and the experiences of someone else. We cannot be certain how they feel or how they should feel just because we believe that we have been through the same things they have. Possibly, the circumstances are the same, but the intensity of the challenges or joys can be more or less, and even if they were exactly the same, our reactions are what make up each personal situation.

21

A CLEAR CONSCIENCE

As usual, the telephone in our house sounded insistently while I was busy feeding the baby. I closed my eyes for a moment and sighed, restraining the impulse to run and answer the call. If it was something urgent, they would leave me a message or they would call my cell phone, which was always close to me. With three small children, it was difficult to run to take calls, plus most of the time I did not know where I had left the phone after using it.

That was one of the reasons why I loved having caller ID at home: if someone did not leave a message, I had the ability to check the number, and if it seemed important, I would call back. I no longer had to go through the same experience of previous years when many times I stopped doing something important, ran to the phone, and in the end, did not arrive in time or found it was someone who was just trying to sell something.

Now when I receive a phone call where I do not recognize the caller's number or voice, and the person does not identify themselves, my immediate reaction is to hang up, even if they ask for me by name. If I ask who is calling and they answer me with the question, "You do not know who I am?!" then my patience is tried. This is one of those questions that I think is perfect for a guessing game where the person gives some data or clues to know who is being talked about, but it is an inadequate question when making a phone call.

What goes through my head at that moment is, *"No, I do not know who you are; that's why I asked for your name. And if I'm going to lose some important minutes of my life, you have two seconds to let me know if I actually want to talk to you."* Well, I don't actually speak those words, as I'm never sure if I really want to know who is calling me, but I do I give them another two seconds before hanging up!

That day, when the baby finally fell asleep after eating, I told my other two children to leave the room without making a sound, so as not to wake her up. As I placed her gently in her cradle, I heard the phone ring once more. I walked on tiptoe when I left the room, and when I closed the door, I knew I had lost the call again. I went to the kitchen to find out who had been trying to call me. I checked the phone, and as I did not find a number that was familiar or a message left for me, I forgot about it.

After dinner, while my husband was entertaining the children, I heard the phone ring again. This time, I ran to answer it, knowing that at that time of night they were usually not calling me to sell me something or to invite me to be part of a survey.

When I heard the voice on the other side of the phone, it seemed very strange that the person hesitated when asking for me by using my maiden name, which I had not used for more than ten years. Thinking they were looking for someone else, I asked the common question, "Who is this?"

A male voice answered, "It's me. You do not know who I am?!"

I tried to tell if the voice was one of my brothers trying to joke with me. When I realized that it was not one of them, I was about to hang up, but I remembered my rule and gave them two more seconds. "Who?" I asked again.

"Your conscience" was the response I received. Unable to avoid it, I laughed at the idea that someone either knew me very well to joke in that way or really had the wrong number.

My husband wondered who was calling; I covered the speaker and told him with a grin on my face, "He says it's my conscience!" He laughed, and I sat next to him while the children were still entertained.

Now there were two of us who were intrigued to know who this mysterious person was. I put the phone on speaker, and then I asked without thinking about the risks, "And what memories does my conscience have of me?"

First, he mentioned the name of a place where my husband and I had been before, and therefore I imagined that we both knew who was calling. But when the voice said the names of two people, my husband indicated that he did not know them—but I did. The voice described a particular scenario that I experienced when I was seventeen years old. Hearing the unmistakable laughter on the other side of the phone, I said, "Juan, how are you?!" After that question, many others followed. I met Juan during my wonderful years of adolescence, and although it had been a long time since then, I felt very happy to hear from him again.

I was grateful to have had the patience to give two more seconds after the question "You do not know who I am?" Well, if I had let the anger grow when I thought, "No, I do not know who you are; that's why I am asking for your name," it would have prevented me from continuing with the game of riddles, and I would have missed the opportunity to share a few minutes with my "conscience." I know there are words that should never be spoken even when there are things that we do not like, because they would surely be remembered as unpleasant. We could give a thousand excuses to justify them, but it would be difficult to erase them from the mind of another person. And if that person acts as our conscience, someday he will mention it to us.

After hanging up the phone, I laughed at my husband when he said, "It's good that your conscience reminded you that you've lived and done nice things and not moments that you feel ashamed of! I like that you are not afraid to let your conscience speak out loud and let me listen to it!" At that moment I realized that even if I had not put the call on speaker, the truth about the moments and things that I have lived throughout my life cannot be kept hidden. Although I do not say it out loud or with the desire for someone to listen to it, I am the set of my choices, decisions, and moments lived. If someone else was present at some point, like my "conscience," that person remembers it.

Every time I have the opportunity to see or converse with Juan, I remember how important it is to do and say what we want to be remembered by. I think the phrase *"I have a clear conscience"* should not only apply to what we think about ourselves, but what others think of us. Although we sometimes declare that what others think is not important, we can breathe a little easier when the consciences of those we know can affirm that the two seconds that they had shared their existence with us have been worth it.

22

ASK THE ONE WHO KNOWS

Something I had wished to do for many years was to get back on a train. The only time I had gone on one before was when I was very small, and I think I enjoyed it a lot, so I wanted to repeat the adventure. After fulfilling my wish, I cannot say that I regretted it, but I promised not to do it again or at least not for such a long trip.

The trip lasted more than thirty-six hours, and it was entertaining at first, but as time went on, I began to doubt that it had been a good idea. It was exciting to see the vendors who offered food or art at each stop. My husband asked me many times if I was sure I wanted to do the same route as when I was a child. I answered "yes" every time.

Many years had passed since I had lived in the country where I was born, so the opportunity to go back and visit was important to me. People still traveled as I remembered: with family, boxes, and suitcases at their sides. I did not remember the way the seats got hard after a few hours or that the heating was inadequate, causing the inside of the train to always be cold. The only thing that had changed in more than twenty years was my age. But I had planned to enjoy the trip, and those little details were not going to stop me from doing just that.

The first night was exciting. Although we could not get a full night's sleep, I was happy to make the time pass by sharing with my husband some of the anecdotes I remembered from when I was a child. The next morning, different landscapes began to appear, and at first I thought they were wonderful, but over time they became monotonous. A few seats ahead of me, I saw a family with a group of children who had entered the train a couple of hours earlier that morning and were playing cards. I tried to read a little while my husband took a nap, and without realizing it, I too fell asleep despite the noise.

When I woke up, I once again became bored. The family a few seats ahead of me again caught my attention, and I realized that the children were busy with other things, so I decided to ask them if they could lend me their card game. They kindly told me yes, and that I could keep the cards because they were going to arrive at their destination in fifteen minutes. One of the children was about my size, so I offered him one of my sweatshirts in return. The dad said, "No," but the boy jumped out in excitement and in the end we made a deal. I stayed with the game, and the boy got off the train wearing my blue jacket.

My brothers and I learned to play cards from an early age. My father was a good teacher—he always told us that a card game is not won only because one is lucky, but because he has used a certain intelligence. The challenge for us was to show who paid the most attention to come out victorious. We had certain rules: Do not fight, do not cheat, and above all, accept that you do not always win, so getting angry is not an option. It was always fun to play with my brothers until we realized that this was not exactly a game for children. For years I saw my dad play solo, and that's the way I learned to play. That night, after many years of not playing cards, I placed the cards in a seat in front of me and started to get rid of my boredom.

It had only been a few minutes when I felt someone standing next to me. I thought it was my husband, but upon seeing that it was actually two women, I picked up the cards from the seat, thinking they wanted to sit there. They smiled and asked if I could read the cards for them. For a moment I did not understand what they were saying, but when I realized what they thought I was doing, I laughed and said that I was just playing a game. One of them told me, "Please read them to me. I'll even pay you. I need to know some things about my future." Again I laughed and explained that I did not read cards, that I only played with them and that I forgot how to even use them. I suddenly heard my husband's laughter. He told the women that I was not a gypsy, although it seemed that way.

With a serious face, the woman again addressed me, ignoring the presence of my husband, and asked me, "You do not believe that someone can tell you their future by reading the cards?"

"No," I answered shortly.

Then I heard the voice of the woman who had not spoken before: "When I was a young girl, a lady read them to me and said that I was going to get married, that I was going to have a lot of happiness, but that I would experience great sadness. I have gone through that, because not long ago my husband died. I want to know what's going to happen next."

As my husband settled into the seat next to me, I was grateful he took me by the hand, because he and I felt that what she wanted to hear was someone to give her hope that the days to come would be better.

Seeing the pain and desperation on her face, I invited her to sit in front of me. I explained again that I did not believe that someone could tell us the future in that way, that what the "fortune teller" had mentioned to her many years ago was something that we all live through. Moments of sadness, moments of joy, moments of laughter, and moments of mourning. "There is something that is certain," I said. "We can all live with the hope that we will always receive new opportunities to improve our lives. Happiness is not only when we enjoy what is pleasant, but when we know that even despite the difficult times, we are doing the right thing."

She looked at me through eyes filled with grief and asked, "Do you believe that I will stop feeling this pain?"

"I don't know if the pain will disappear, but it will surely be less intense as time passes."

As she got up from the seat, she asked me again, "So, you still don't think there's someone who can tell me what I need to do and what's going to happen next?"

"Yes," I answered, pointing to the blue sky out the window. "He knows. Ask Him."

Many of us also want to find someone to tell us what will happen tomorrow in our lives. Someone who can answer our questions, solve our problems, and teach us how to achieve tranquility and happiness. Undoubtedly, there are also many who—even though they have their own unanswered questions, their own unresolved challenges, and are looking for their own stability, joy, or well-being—are willing to give us advice. They may have the best intentions of helping us, but their wisdom is limited.

If we need consolation, guidance, understanding, and instruction on how to direct our lives, all we have to do is ask. Ask the one who knows us, who loves us, and who can help us change our lives. Let's ask Him.

23

DISCOVERING OUR EMOTIONS

Friday evenings are the nights my husband and I set aside and enjoy going out for a few hours together. After so many years, our children do not ask if we will go out; rather, they ask what we will do or where we are going in case they do not find us at home.

"Where do you want to go? What movie do you want to see? Where do you want to eat dinner?" These are the questions my husband constantly asks, and my answer is always, "Whatever you want is fine! I like everything." Again the question comes: "Do you want Mexican, Italian, Chinese, or Thai food?" To which I respond at random, "Italian food!" And of course, after a few seconds of silence, I hear his voice saying, "Are you sure you don't want Mexican food?" In my mind, I assume that's what he wants, and as I really do not have a preference, I mention the restaurant we like where they offer that kind of food. After a very short silence, I will hear his voice again assuring me that we have not been to the Chinese restaurant for a long time and that today is possibly a good day to go. In the end, we could save time and skip the questions that come after the first one, if—instead of listening to my answer—he could read my expression, which says, *"I know that we always end up going to the place where you think I would like more, and I am happy about that."*

On one particular evening, he assured me there was a place I would love, as one of his co-workers had recommended it. I told him that I had also heard from someone else about that restaurant, but the recommendation was that we should avoid eating there. In the end we decided that we should form our own opinion about the restaurant. Coincidentally, that evening we did not go alone on our weekly date; we had planned to go out with another couple. The four of us ventured out to the new restaurant.

When we arrived, we realized that many people had the same idea as us. We waited about thirty minutes to be seated. While standing by other people, I noticed that almost none of them were talking, but I observed that they felt the same as us—desperation, hunger, and a bit of boredom from the wait. When it was finally our turn, we took a few minutes to review the menu and ordered quickly because we were ready to eat. We still had to wait a bit, but we were happy when our plates with food arrived at our table.

During the evening, our conversations fluctuated among many topics, and as we were situated between two tables, we realized that each table was speaking in a different language. We guessed that one group was speaking in Japanese, although we didn't know with certainty because none of us understood it. The other group we could understand because they were conversing in English. Our group was talking in Spanish. My husband, my friend, and I were born in Mexico, and my friend's husband was born in Germany, but he had learned to speak Spanish and she had learned to speak German.

The abundance of different languages spoken that night was a subject that we could not pass up. The important thing was to be able to express what we wanted in the language in which we could be understood. We laughed, saying that was the reason my husband and I argued in Spanish and why, as my friend had lived in Germany for more than twenty years, she and her husband "fixed their differences" in German.

At none of the tables did we notice any inconvenience when communicating with one another. We asked the waitress if she spoke a different language than English. She didn't, and explained that even though many people spoke various languages, no one seemed to have a problem addressing her.

While tasting our dinner, our opinions varied as to whether we liked it or not. Each one gave an opinion, but recognizing that our palates and tastes are different, we decided that it was a place to which we would like to return. The tables were so close together that we could hear whenever someone in one of the other groups shared a joke, because everyone was laughing. When we were almost finished with our desserts and just as they were leaving, a child began to cry at the table where they spoke a language we did not recognize.

It was exciting to discover in those moments that, even though we speak different languages and our tastes for a certain type of food can vary, there is something that cannot be misunderstood: our gestures and our emotions. We can call things different names or have different intonations, but feelings and expressions do not change. When we laugh or cry, we do not let others discover where we are from or what language we are most comfortable expressing ourselves with. Cries or laughter always have the same sound. Despair and boredom can be discovered without uttering words, and joy can be read in our faces even when we remain in total silence.

From that moment on, I understood that we can speak the same or a different language, and if our thinking, knowledge, or opinions are different, there is something that we can never hide or fail to notice: the happiness or pain that those around us are going through. Laughter or pain does not need translation, and if we pay attention, it may not even be necessary to listen to the sound to understand those feelings.

24

DO I KNOW YOU?

After passing the same gas station for the third time, I realized I was driving in circles, so I decided to park. While sitting in my car with a map in my hands and trying not to lose patience after all the time I had wasted, I tried again to find my way to my destination. It was 2002, and GPS was not a common tool yet. When I saw a small convenience store ahead, I decided to ask the cashier for directions.

Before turning the car on again, I closed my eyes and took a deep breath, knowing that what I was doing was for a good cause. My friend Sandra's cry for help that morning came to mind. She called to tell me that while reviewing some documents, she had found an address with the name of her cousin. She had completely lost contact with her cousin because the phone number she used to call her on had been disconnected.

My friend explained, "I know that these are very busy days for you, but it will not take you more than an hour to find out if my cousin, Maggie, still lives at the same address."

I smiled while I remembered the last time I had seen Sandra. Eight years without seeing her did not feel that long when maintaining a friendship through letters, calls, and messages. In just a few more days, she would be back home after living in another country and I was incredibly happy. After finishing our conversation, I mentally went through my plans for the day. Before leaving my house, I made sure that my map of the city was in the glove compartment of my car.

The man at the convenience store explained to me that I was only a couple blocks away from my destination. When turning left on the correct street, I drove slowly to try and find the right house number. A couple of times I had to step out of my car to check the mailbox closely because the house number was faded. I finally found the house I was searching for and prayed that the person I was looking for still lived in that home.

When I made sure there were no dogs trying to bite me, I approached the front door and rang the doorbell. After several attempts with no answer, I began to make my way back to my car when the front door slowly opened. I saw a woman with her hair pulled back, wearing a robe and not even a drop of makeup. I realized that my insistent knocking and doorbell ringing had woken her up. I apologized quickly and explained why I was there. As soon as I mentioned Sandra's name, the eyes of the lady lit up. That was enough confirmation for me to know she was the one I was looking for.

I told her what my friend had told me, and although we exchanged a few words, I knew that I should leave, since she worked graveyard shifts and had only arrived home a couple hours before. Maggie had to repeat a couple of times her desire to have my friend's new number, because my thoughts had already moved onto figuring out how to get back in time to pick up my son from school.

After I said goodbye, Maggie promised me that she would be at the welcome reception in honor of my friend's husband that following week. The company where he had worked for the past twenty years offered him a management position that would allow them to return to the same city they had left eight years ago.

At home later that day, I had already forgotten about my little adventure that morning. I did not call Sandra to tell her that I had accomplished what she asked. I knew she would be very busy because of the move. Besides, I thought that she had probably already received a call from her cousin that confirmed that my mission had been fulfilled.

On the Friday night of the following week, my husband and I arrived at the welcome reception where we would see our friends again. There was soft music playing in the background, and people were talking amongst each other. I could see through a window that my dear friend looked radiant. When our eyes met, we ran without hesitation to embrace each other after many years of being apart.

We only had a couple of minutes to exchange words and smiles, because several people gathered around us to greet her as well. At that moment, I noticed that there was a very attractive woman whom Sandra had been speaking to when I arrived. We were about to greet each other when our friends told us to follow them to a table. Time passed quickly between dinner, stories about living abroad, and stories about the past.

After dessert, I asked the woman sitting next to my friend if she also worked for the same company or if they had known each other for a long time. The silence that followed my question told me that something was wrong. I turned my head from one side to another without knowing what was happening.

Finally, a great laugh interrupted the silence. Sandra explained to me, with laughter in her voice, that she had not introduced us, thinking that we already knew each other. I became very confused because I was sure that I had never met the woman sitting by her. I observed the woman carefully and asked her, "Do I know you?" With some disbelief, she answered that she had had the pleasure of meeting me a few days before and that, thanks to me, she had been able to see *her cousin* again.

I do not know what shade of red my face was or how long I was speechless. My eyes and mouth opened wide with surprise as I recognized the woman standing in front me. She was the woman who opened the door in robe a week before. I apologized quickly, feeling embarrassed by my lack of memory, because I was so distracted with my never-ending to-do list, that even though I saw and talked with Sandra's cousin, I never really paid attention to her.

It would be very easy for me to use the excuse that she was unrecognizable because of the way she was dressed a week before or the makeup she was wearing now, but the truth is that I never noticed the color of her eyes or her hair. I did not take a moment to register in my mind the features of her face or the tone of her voice. I could not even recall her height or her age. I was so absorbed in my own daily challenges that I forgot to pay attention to the person standing right in front of me. I realized that many times we look but do not see. We sometimes look at someone or something, but we do not imprint in our minds or in our hearts the details of the things that our eyes can see.

The lesson I learned with Maggie is not that we should try to remember every detail of a person so that when we meet them we can avoid embarrassment later on. Rather, that experience helped me understand that our lack of perception prevents us from recognizing certain opportunities. Because we are out of time or lack interest, we do not identify them. We spend time looking for possibilities to reach our goals, and we ask those who have experience or knowledge for help, which is the easiest or fastest way to get there. Yet when opportunity opens its doors, we are so busy that we do not pay attention or recognize it for what it really is.

If we do not pay attention, we will go through this life with excuses as to why we stumble or make mistakes that could have been avoided, and we will let opportunities that could improve our lives slip right past us without even realizing they were there to begin with.

25

LEARN TO SWIM, DON'T DROWN

Do we need hard challenges to learn some lessons, or do we need to learn some lessons before facing hard challenges?

After coming back from a conference at her school, my fourteen-year-old daughter asked me, "Mom, if I want to succeed in life, do I need to go through a big challenge first?" She explained that every time she had the opportunity to hear a motivational speaker who is successful, they always talked about when they faced the worst time in their lives.

I asked her what her opinion was. She just looked at me in confusion, saying that the lady that spoke in the last conference she attended said that her success was based on the fact that she had a big accident, and other speakers talked about poverty, sickness, rejection, or the death of a loved one. With a fearful expression, my girl said, "If I need to go through something like them, I am not sure that I want to be successful!"

I knew this was one of those moments that I call "teaching time," and after a quick personal prayer in my mind, I started to tell her how I found an answer to the same question.

When I was six years old, my parents decided to move the whole family to a city in southern Mexico, thinking that they could have more opportunities to work and provide a better living for us. After spending my life in a place surrounded by a desert where my face was always dry in winter and in summer, I felt blessed when we began a new life in a place known as *The City of the Eternal Spring*. As the name implied, the weather was just perfect.

A week after we arrived, we asked my dad if we could play baseball, a sport that we usually played in our old town. He told us that it was time to learn a new sport. He said, "Where we lived before, you needed protection from the sun, so I taught you to play baseball with a hat on. Here, with all these rivers, lakes, and pools, you need to learn how to swim." We knew that if Dad said it, it was going to happen. We felt happy to start a new adventure. For me it meant, "Goodbye, baseball caps; hello, bathing suits!"

There were six children, and my dad didn't have the money for us to take swimming lessons, so he looked for the closest place with water to start teaching us this new sport. Behind our home was an irrigation canal. The current was unusually strong, but my father came up with a great idea to combat the current. He tied three ropes across the canal and then instructed us to jump in. He told us that as soon our feet touched the ground, we needed to push ourselves out and reach one of the three ropes. My father advised us to take deep breaths and jump until we could reach a rope. In my eyes, he was an expert, because in my family, he was the only one that knew how to swim. He was born in that region, and when he said that we needed to learn how to swim, it was because he knew it was necessary for our survival.

Even my younger brothers were brave enough to give it a try as soon as the instructions were given. I stood close to the edge, but when I saw how fast the water was moving, I shook my head and started backing away. My dad placed his hand on my shoulder and encouraged me to jump. He said, "Sooner or later you are going to learn, and it is going to be better if it is sooner rather than later. With all these rivers and lakes surrounding us, the time to learn how to swim is now before you drown."

And then ... I jumped.

Water filled my mouth as I came up for air, and I began to panic as I tried reaching the first rope without success. I heard my father's voice say, *"Breathe, jump, and get the rope!"* but I missed the second one, too. I opened my eyes, trying to see the third and last rope. This was my last chance before I would be swept down the canal in the fast-moving current. At one moment I felt that I had missed my last opportunity, discouraging me from jumping anymore. When I started swallowing water, my instinct to survive kicked in, and just before I ran out of air, I grabbed it! I felt victorious. I felt capable. I felt happy when I saw my dad's eyes full of pride.

After a few days, we didn't need the ropes anymore. We learned how to swim in an intense environment. This new skill brought many happy moments in our lives and peace of mind to my parents. During my childhood and adolescent years, I enjoyed swimming with confidence in all the lakes, rivers, and pools that we had access to.

After telling this childhood story to my daughter, I concluded by telling her that everyone faces different challenges in this life. We have the tendency to think ours are the hardest and that other people have a better and happier life. We need to choose for ourselves if we need hard challenges to learn some lessons or if we need to learn some lessons before facing hard challenges. The results are going to be different depending on what we choose, but it is up to us to choose what is right for us.

I explained to her that the probability to learn, do better, and set new goals after a tragic experience is higher, but many times we don't have the opportunity. When she asked me why not, I told her that she needed to remember her cousin, Brian, who was only four years old when he tragically passed away. He was having a great Fourth of July day in a pool and always wore a life jacket. That day after having lunch, he forgot to put it back on, and he didn't know how to swim. When his parents saw his body floating in the water, it was too late. My daughter sadly said, "You are right, Mom. He didn't have the opportunity to develop this skill, because he didn't have time."

I want all my children to understand that they don't need to feel guilty if they don't face extreme situations and that being successful is not always a result of going through hard challenges. I want them to clearly understand that we are all going to have difficulties in our lives, and they need to learn how to come out victorious.

As my father said about swimming, *"Sooner or later you are going to learn, and it is going to be better if it is sooner rather than later."* With all these obstacles and difficulties surrounding us, the time to learn how to face them is now before you suffer more. We need to jump, breathe, and survive!

Adversity is essential to our eternal progress. However, each of us must decide for ourselves how to deal with adversity and when to be prepared.

I told my daughter, "You can be successful when you decide it; don't let the challenges decide for you. Learn to swim, don't drown. You still have the chance."

26

LOOKING FOR THE BEST SECTION!

The bus was almost full of young people waiting to have fun for a whole week at a conference that would take place near the beach. As incredible as it seemed, we were all at the meeting spot on time. We decided to meet at 7:30 in the evening to make sure we could leave right at eight o'clock. An hour later, we stopped to pick up a group from a different school who shared the expenses of the bus rental.

We would travel all night, because the next morning we had to be at the university where the conference was taking place. Of course, each of us knew that these were just some of the opportunities we would have to be in contact with people who had our same aspirations. To be realistic, though, I don't think that it was more important than being with friends and exploring new places.

With the exception of a few, most of us still lived in our parents' house, and though we were all considered adults, we were not yet self-sufficient. At home there were rules to follow, and like most young people, many of us thought that those rules did not apply in a different place. The seats in the bus were not assigned, but we all knew it was divided into three sections: those who wanted to sleep sat in the front, those who were going to talk sat in the middle, and those who did not want to be disturbed sat in the back. Our parents were not there to help us know which section was the best. Even when we wanted some freedom, my friends and I chose to sit almost at the beginning of the second section, because we knew that after a couple hours of talking, we would be ready to sleep.

During those days away from home, the only rules that applied were "don't judge" and "don't pressure anyone to do what they do not want to do." We all agreed, so if someone wanted to change sections throughout the trip, all they had to do was find an available spot.

The next morning, we took a few minutes to settle into the hotel and then arrived on time at the auditorium where our first conference would take place. We continued with the same rules at the auditorium. No, not the one of not judging or pressing, but the one for the sections on the bus. The front seats in the auditorium were occupied for those that were awake and ready to listen. In the middle were those who never stopped talking. In the back were all those who wore sunglasses, not to cover their eyes from the sun, but to hide the traces of sleeplessness from the night before. Undoubtedly, even though all the students were from different parts of the country, we knew where our place was.

DURING THE DAYS THAT FOLLOWED, we visited many places and enjoyed different activities. There were dinners, dances, and visits to factories and companies. We listened to successful people in the field of chemical engineering, and of course, we enjoyed our visit to the beaches and historical places.

None of us complained that these trips were unnecessary. Our only discontent was that they were not frequent enough or that we did not have the money to participate. Attending many classes together and events like this helped us to develop respect for one another. There were many times we had different points of view and did not always make the same decisions, yet we supported each other because we respected one another. There was always someone who was willing to help with homework, to solve problems, or to share lunch. Those times, like many others in my life, were wonderful years.

As always at the end of certain cycles, all of us grew in different directions. I moved, and like my classmates, I became an adult. Those days were replaced by days of greater responsibility. I got married and had children.

I grew up in a home where I learned that I had to respect others, but mainly to respect the principles that I had been taught. I have tried to continue doing what I know makes me happy, which in turn saves me a lot of headaches. I would be lying if I said that I have never made mistakes, but now my task is to teach my children what has helped me.

One day, having four children at home, I was invited to speak about parenting, and I was surprised at the end of the conference to find someone who said he had met me during one of the trips in my youth. He told me that he came with a second group of students, and he remembers hearing the conversation between my friends and me for much of the night. When introducing me to his wife, he joked by saying about me, "She has been practicing the art of talking for more than twenty years." After a brief explanation of how he had met me, I imagined that he had already told her about what had happened on the bus, because he mentioned, "She sat in the second section." When I asked him where he had sat, his answer was, "In the best one!" Someone else interrupted us, and I did not have time to ask him which section he was referring to.

I think we can all differ as to which is the best section at a certain time in our lives. If you are one of those who prefer to have a quiet life and always be alert, you will decide on the first section. If you like to talk and try to solve problems, even though many times you have no idea which is the best solution, you will surely feel happy in the second section. But if you like to celebrate, do not always follow the conventional rules, and sometimes hide the consequences of something that was not right, you will say that the last section is where you belong. I think I continue to stay in the second section, sometimes closer to the first one and other times closer to the third. I know people who were in the first and moved from there, others who were in the third and have moved to a different one. I know we all have the freedom to move sections if we feel uncomfortable.

We will not always have someone to tell us which is the best section, or often we do not want to hear someone else's suggestion. We must never forget the rule to not judge and not put pressure on those who do not share our point of view. Instead, we should be ready to help whoever is in need.

In the end, the most important thing is to realize that the bus that we call life is something we will always have to share. The seats are not assigned, and no matter our age, we have to make our own decision where to sit.

27

OUT OF TUNE

M usic has always been an important part of my life. I would like to be able to say that my voice is extraordinarily melodious or that my talent in playing certain instruments is incredible, but it is not so. I do not have a privileged voice, and my only attempt in learning to play an instrument was when I was a teenager. My neighbor, who was two years older than me, played the guitar, and I thought that could be a way for him to notice that I existed. But as soon as I realized that my fingers ached when pressing the strings, I simply gave up.

The only reason I've enjoyed music is that since I was born, if the radio was not turned on to my dad's favorite station, he would sing all the songs that played on the station all day. As time passed, my interest was not the songs my father listened to, but the ones I could dance to at parties. At nineteen, I met a lady who played the piano and who loved classical music. The difference between classical and the regular music I listened to was enormous, but I liked it and enjoyed both types of music.

One of my personal challenges is to learn about the things that someone else finds important. So, I dedicated myself to reading about the lives of great classical music composers. I read about four composers whom I considered the most famous, and that was enough for me. I have never had a good ear, so I memorized the names of some of their compositions, just in case a conversation about them came up.

A few years ago, I lived in a city where a small group of people with beautiful voices attended the same church as I did. It was always a delight to hear them sing. One of my friends was part of that group. Once, while I was standing beside her, someone approached her to invite her to sing in a special program. She accepted, saying the names of those who would accompany her. The person who spoke with her turned to me and said, "I hope you can also join us." I smiled, and before I could answer, my friend quickly told him, "If you want it to be something nice, we better invite her to just listen!" The man was a little embarrassed, so I clarified that what she had said was completely true; singing was not an option for me, and everyone who knew me understood that.

Weeks later, I had the opportunity to attend the program and to listen to the musical number they had prepared for that night. I realized that something was going terribly wrong. Without having much idea about musical notes, I knew that somehow the music did not sound pleasant or at least not what we were accustomed to when they sang. When the program finished and I approached the group, I could see that they were ashamed. As I hugged my friend, I told her that next time everything would be as it always had been. She told me, "Next time you will sing with us, so we will have someone to blame if something goes wrong!" Those words made everyone laugh and forget for a moment the bad time they had just experienced.

We all have different talents; we have developed different skills or acquired greater knowledge in certain areas. We cannot hide that a talent or skill will never be natural to us, and we know there are others that we could learn, but we just haven't yet. We should not feel less important or inadequate when we are not part of certain groups. It doesn't mean that our understanding, grace, or instruction does not match others or that we are not accepted. We cannot always be in tune with everything that surrounds us. Without a doubt, we can all put

more effort into learning more about what interests us or at least have
an idea about issues that are important. I appreciate that music can be
a part of those who listen to it, compose it, play it, or even dance to it.
Each of us can enjoy it, just like many other things in this life. And if
times arise when our talent does not go as expected, we can be
assured that there will always be other opportunities to shine.

28

RECEIVING HELP

After two years of living in a new place, life again began to take on a sense of normality. We had moved to a city where we did not know anyone but the family of one of my husband's co-workers who had also moved because of work.

Our family and friends of many years had stayed in the city where we had lived in for a long time. The process of adaptation had been difficult for me. The days seemed to drag on and felt routine. The only times the phone rang was when family members called to know how we were. Yet I slowly began to discover that in this new place as well as in others, the only thing I needed was to find a way to help those around me and to feel involved in the community.

I decided to volunteer at my son's school, where I could take home papers to cut and projects to organize in bags. They asked me if I could collaborate in some activities, and it seemed like another way to help. I could not spend much time in the classroom because I had a newborn baby, and it was almost inevitable that her crying would interrupt the class. Either way, that was an opportunity for me to feel like I was doing something for someone else and to meet other people.

Without realizing it, the person I was actually helping was me. The days passed too quickly, and there were always things to do. One day I received a call from a father of one of my son's classmates, asking if I could pick up his child after school. He explained to me that he was with his wife in the hospital because they just had a baby. She, like me, had no family around, so I decided to go to the hospital to visit her after my husband returned home to stay with the children.

That afternoon, when I arrived at the small hospital, I found a pregnant woman in the hallway asking me if I spoke Spanish. I said yes, and she asked me to help her because there was no one there who could understand what she was trying to say. I went to the receptionist, and in my imperfect English, I started translating. The receptionist explained that she had already told the lady to come back in the morning. The lady then said in a very soft voice, "I want to have the baby here, not in my house." I asked her if she had had any contractions yet, and she said yes. She had been feeling contractions since dawn, and even though she thought the pain would pass, she strongly felt that the baby would be born today. I looked at her with some disbelief, because she showed no signs of pain. I explained the situation to the receptionist, and she started asking many more questions and called a nurse. In a few minutes they were taking the woman to a room, so I once again began to look for the mother of my son's friend.

However, the pregnant woman asked me to call her house to explain what was happening. She gave me her phone number, and when I went to the counter to make the call, I saw people running to her room. I waited a couple of minutes, and then I knew that the baby was born. I asked the receptionist if everything was fine, and she smiled and told me that things were more than well and that she wished there were more births like that.

I made the call, looked for the room of the mother who I had originally came to visit, and saw her beautiful baby. I spent a few minutes with them while assuring them that her son was well at my home.

When I left the room, I asked one of the nurses if I could see the woman I had translated for. They allowed me to pass, and when I was there, I saw a very happy woman with a beautiful baby in her arms who thanked me for my help.

While driving back home and reflecting on these experiences, I began to understand that giving help does not mean we have more money or more time, or that we are better than someone else. I noticed that in my life, the saying *"It is better to give than to receive."* is true because when I give, I receive happiness, gratitude, peace, and above all, the confirmation of knowing that my life has a reason for being.

That afternoon, I had been offered opportunities to help others. I thought that even if I had not been at the hospital, that baby would have been born, but the mother would not have been able to explain the situation to the hospital staff if I hadn't been there to translate. And if I had not picked up my son's friend from school to bring him home while his parents were in the hospital, someone else might have. If we do not make the decision to help, we miss the opportunity to receive.

29

SALT AND PEPPER

My friend Sonia was a beautiful girl; she had dark curly hair that all of us admired. During recess, her hair would shine beautifully in the sun. Even though Sonia knew that everyone dreamed of having hair like hers, she never made us feel like she was more privileged because of it. Instead, she told us that it was better to have straight hair like ours, because it was easier to tame and keep in place.

We were a group of friends with lots of differences, but we loved being with each other. After the weekend, we would reunite at school and share the adventures we had experienced over the previous few days. You could never tell if one of us was telling the truth or if we had made something up, but we all had a chance to be in the spotlight.

After a couple of years being in the same class, we had set some rules. One of our rules was that we each needed to listen when it wasn't our turn to share. Even if we wanted to make a comment, we couldn't interrupt one another or give an opinion until the person telling her story was finished. We decided this rule was necessary because sometimes the thirty minutes we had for recess was just enough to hear the whole story. The questions and opinions could wait until the following days.

Our times together were magical moments because we enjoyed our friendship. It was forbidden to talk about what our conversations were with someone outside of the group. We learned this lesson since our friend, Veronica, got in trouble when she told us that her parents were divorcing. The girls in the group did not keep the secret, and her mom found out. This was a moment and a rule that we needed to remind each other about frequently, because sometimes it was hard for all of us to keep it!

On a typical Monday morning, it was Sonia's turn to report about her weekend adventures. All three of us were attentive and ready to hear her story. We were around eleven years old and had begun showing an interest in boys. Sonia had a crush on our classmate Pedro, which is why we couldn't have anything to do with him during the time that she showed interest in him. It was Sonia who set up this rule.

Sonia began her story by saying, "My aunt and uncle came to visit us, and they brought my mom a wonderful gift. It is the most beautiful thing I have ever seen. Would you like to guess what it is?"

We all eagerly shouted our guesses. "A bracelet? A painting? Flowers? A dress? A puppy?"

"No!" she responded.

"A kitten? A necklace? A music box? Shoes? A purse?"

"No! Don't any of you girls have some imagination?!" Sonia said.

We all were a bit confused, but none of us gave up. We asked for a clue: "Where can it be used?"

Sonia replied, "In the kitchen."

None of us imagined that something so beautiful could be used in the kitchen, but we kept on guessing. "A cookie sheet?!" said Veronica, thinking that she had guessed it because Sonia loved to bake.

"No, not a cookie sheet," Sonia answered.

"I know, I know!" Angelica said. "Plates with flowers painted on them!"

"Nope, not that either."

Finally, it was my turn. It was common knowledge that my role in any kitchen was to eat instead of bake or cook. For that reason, I would never think that an object as beautiful as Sonia was describing could be found in any kitchen. Perhaps what she was describing was as beautiful as it was delicious! I quickly guessed, "A cake!"

Sonia looked at me with a smile and told me, "You are always thinking of food!" We all laughed, knowing that this was not a lie.

We were waiting for her answer, which we knew would come eventually after giving us some details. "Pedro and I were in the same group in math class, and together we solved one of the most difficult problems. I could feel that he was looking at me in a special way, so I think that he likes me." I thought to myself, *Obviously, who wouldn't like Sonia, but what does this have to do with her mom's gift?* I knew I had to wait, though, because that was the rule: No interrupting.

She continued, saying, "I got to the house, and when I saw them on the table, I knew that it was true, Pedro likes me!" We looked at each other—again confused—and at that point we wanted to scream, "What did you see?!" But we restrained ourselves because we knew that it was her special time. It was her moment. In silence, we listened to the rest of her story, even though we were desperate to know what she liked so much and what was on her table.

Sonia went on. "I could've taken a flower and picked off its petals, saying, 'He likes me, he doesn't like me,' to figure it out, but there was no reason to do it because with the gift that was on the table, I don't have a doubt that he likes me."

Not being able to hold it back anymore, all three of us yelled, "What is it!?"

Finally she explained. "They are two small ceramic strawberries with multiple holes at the top of each one. One with an 'S' and the other with a 'P' on the side of each strawberry. Those letters obviously stand for Sonia and Pedro!"

We laughed. It was true what she told us: it was beautiful, romantic, and something none of us would have ever guessed. No, they were not containers for salt and pepper; they were the symbol that Pedro had a crush on Sonia.

After many years, I still enjoy thinking back to that moment. Now every time that I see an "S" and a "P" on my table, it reminds me that if we want friendship to remain and last, no matter the age, imagination and respect need to exist. We need to accept that each one of us has a different perspective on life; that we need to celebrate and laugh together, share our adventures, and—most importantly—keep our secrets.

30

SOLUTIONS

"If you two don't go to bed soon, you're going to have to take your conversation outside, because I'm going to work tomorrow!" It was the voice of Francis's father. That was the third time we heard him say that phrase, and although we knew that our voices and laughter were more audible as the night progressed, we continued with our talk as if we had not heard him.

Our final chemistry exam was the next morning, and we had decided to study together at her house that night. Clearly, we did not just dedicate ourselves to studying. Talking about all the things that seemed interesting was also included in any study session.

Around midnight, while we tried to solve the problems not only from our textbooks but also those that the world had in general, we saw my friend's father appear at the door of her bedroom. "Please go to the kitchen to study, and try not to talk so much, because then you won't be able to fall asleep," he told us kindly. Without hesitation, we went downstairs quickly with our hands full of books and notebooks, which we carelessly dropped on the table. Our main purpose, at that time, was to prepare a sandwich and then continue studying ... and, of course, continue our conversation.

We didn't realize how much time had passed until we saw a frowning face at the kitchen door telling us, "I can hear every word from your conversation, and to me it doesn't make any sense, so it's not interesting. Please let me sleep!" We looked surprised, because we thought that the kitchen was a safe and distant place to talk as much as we wanted. "What time do you plan to fall asleep?" was a question that we could not answer exactly.

"We still have a little more to study," we replied vaguely.

"Maybe if you two spoke less to each other, you would be resting right now," we heard him say as he went up the stairs.

When we thought he was already in his bedroom, we giggled, but we were surprised to hear a voice saying, "I can still hear you!" At that moment, I thought that although my friend's parents loved me, it was going to be a while before they would let me return to spend the night. Even so, we could not contain ourselves; we laughed again, but tried to concentrate on what we still needed to review.

We did not notice how much time went by until suddenly, the lights in the kitchen were no longer necessary. Our eyes were a little tired, but we were happy, because we knew that the exam that we would take that morning would not be a big complication. Yes, we had talked a lot, but we studied with the same intensity. (Well, maybe not the exact same intensity!)

We hurriedly went upstairs to take a shower and change, because we did not want to be late for school. It was not necessary to wear makeup or to waste time fixing our hair. The most important thing was to pass the exam.

As we were putting our books in our backpacks, we saw my friend's father. He looked like he was in a good mood, but, he could not hide the fact that he had not slept enough the night before. "Are you two ready to get one of the highest grades?" he asked. We both responded quickly with a yes. "And what about the problems that those around us have? Have you also found a solution?" He asked with a smile; but without saying the words, he was telling us that we'd wasted our time trying to think of solutions.

During breakfast we continued talking, no longer in soft murmurs, because now there was no one we could wake up. As we walked the long road that led us to school, there was not a time when we did not talk or laugh. The sun hurt our eyes, but the morning was beautiful. Very soon, we would be on vacation and happy to have passed our exam.

In our classroom, the teacher began to give us instructions on the exam that we were about to take, but at some point Francis's voice and mine were the only ones that were heard. We did not know at what instant everyone had become silent. "Ladies, I understand perfectly that since you have not seen each other, you have a lot to talk about, but if you allow me, we are going to start the exam." We laughed again at our teacher's words.

After finishing the exam, we met up with my friend's younger sister in the hallway who told us in a sarcastic tone, "Let me interrupt your deep conversation. Do you two ever get tired of talking?!"

We looked surprised, and together we responded, "Noooo!"

"What do you two even talk about so much?" Alejandra continued to ask.

"We talk about everything!"

"And what do you even solve?"

"Nothing," we answered. When we saw her face full of displeasure, we continued walking and chatting.

Few people understand that most of the discussions between friends are not to find solutions to issues. With true friends, there are no uncomfortable silences. Questions are asked, doubts are shared, opinions are held, and different points of view are respected. Conversation is not intended to change the course of the world, but to discuss ways to improve it. Most of the topics analyzed do not have an end. On thousands of occasions, the topics are so trivial that a couple of minutes after the discussion, they have already been forgotten.

What is not forgotten is that each of these friendly arguments has fulfilled its purpose: to make us feel closer and become accomplices. If each problem had only one solution, the discussions between friends would be very brief. But since there are many solutions for each problem, it is necessary to take time to find them. The advantage is that when there is a need for an answer in our lives, after being specialists in almost every argument, we will often know which solution to apply.

31

STEPPING INTO THE PAST

It was a beautiful Sunday morning when I saw her. She was sitting in the front row of the church, and I knew that she was paying attention to the message delivered to the youth. I wondered what she was thinking, because the expression in her eyes was so sweet, and from time to time her lips made a soft curve.

I looked around the room and saw that it was packed. Even though the majority was boys and girls between twelve and eighteen years old, they were quiet and trying to pay attention to the words of the speaker. From time to time, giggles were heard or someone looked distracted, but the important thing was that they were there.

When I turned to pay attention to the words being spoken, I heard a familiar tap on the floor. I paused as the sound brought memories to my mind, and I let my thoughts fly for a second to the time when I was sixteen in a similar meeting. I was sitting beside my best friend, listening to her tennis shoes tapping the floor in the same way.

Many years have passed, but I can recognize that soft sound even when a room is full of people. My friend, Linda, loved to play basketball, and when she received green tennis shoes as a gift one year, she wore them everywhere. They became her trademark, and when she was listening or trying to learn something, she tapped on the floor.

The first few times, like others, I thought that the only thing my friend wanted when she tapped the floor was to call attention to herself or to her tennis shoes—they were beautiful and not very common. As time passed by, I realized that was not true. Linda knew that the gift she had received was expensive and special; it was the reason why she always wore them, because it was a way to show her appreciation.

I realized that the noise she made with her feet was her way of concentrating. Not only did she do it when she was wearing her sneakers or when we were in a church meeting, but when we were studying or ready to play in a basketball game. Many years ago, when someone mentioned that my friend did not pay attention and seemed to be bored, I explained that when she did not show interest in something, it was when we did not hear the soft noise of her shoes tapping against the floor.

My memories faded, and the meeting was over. I approached the girl in the front row and asked her if she played basketball. She said yes, but that the season was over. When I asked her name, she said with a sweet voice, "Amira." I couldn't believe that was her name! This name is uncommon among my culture. I had heard it only once in my life; it was the name of Linda's aunt.

When Amira stood up, I noticed that she was as tall as Linda, and for some strange coincidence, she wore her hair in a bun similar to the way my friend had worn hers in the '80s. It did not surprise me, because somehow the hair pulled up is a distinct style for some women who play sports. I told her my story and shared the memories of my foot-tapping friend with her. She smiled, and I felt I had been transported back to when Linda and I talked about things that mattered in our lives.

I drove back home that Sunday, thinking that many times—without planning—we can leave memories in the people around us with the things we do or say. It is not really important what type of shoes we wear during our lifetime. It doesn't matter if they are beautiful, unique, or special. The most important aspects are the footprints we leave when we are walking in them.

As soon as I entered the house and heard the noise of my high heels against the floor, I challenged myself that the sound of my steps will bring good memories to those who hear them in the future.

32

SWEET, SOUR, & PAINFUL

"Do you realize we look like sisters?" Lucia told me when we had finished sharing a huge slice of watermelon.

"Really?" I replied, looking at her and knowing that no one had ever made such a comment like that before, because we were totally different. She had wavy black hair; I had straight, light brown hair. She was tall and I was much shorter. "We don't look like each other that much, but at least we are the same size in clothes and we surely have the same number of teeth!" I laughed. Even with my clarification and without waiting for her answer, I agreed that we looked like sisters.

I think she caught my momentary doubt, because she still told me her point of view. "Sisters share everything, and you and I, we share everything!"

I looked at the watermelon peel, which only had the white and green colors left since we made the red disappear, and I said with a smile, "It's true; you and I even share watermelon!"

I met Lucia when we were twelve years old. We went to the same school, and as her mother and mine had mall stores very close to each other, we walked there together at the end of classes. It was one of those situations where we did not return directly home after school because our moms practically lived where they worked. Many times, we did our homework together and helped a little before we started playing. We had fun talking with the people who visited the stores. My mom sold prepared food, and Lucia's mom sold the ingredients to prepare a meal. We always laughed at everything. Many times we tried to guess what the next person who passed by the shops would buy. The person who would guess right the most had the pleasure of deciding where to hang out the following Thursday. That was the day when our mothers did not need us nearby since most of the stores were closed, and there were not many people around. Our options were always the movies or swimming; everything depended on the money we had. Our moms did not worry. They knew we were together and close to home.

We had two favorite places in common. One was a shop where they sold fresh fruit juices and smoothies. Laura, the owner, gave us a free treat after helping her out a little. We would remove the orange peels, wash the blender glasses, mop the floor, and throw away the garbage—all in less than ten minutes. My favorite smoothie flavor was mango, Lucia's was strawberry, and although we would ask each other, "How can you like that? Yuck!" we always shared them in the end.

The other place we enjoyed visiting was a magazine stand, where the owner always let us browse if we did some errands and if we were careful and didn't mistreat the magazines in any way. How I liked the smell of fresh paper! But above all, I loved to read. Lucia loved fashion magazines, but I loved magazines with interesting stories, although I was a little disappointed to see that there were more pictures than words, which meant that the end came all too soon.

One afternoon, Lucia was a bit mysterious and told me in a low voice, "I discovered something, but promise me that you will not ask me questions or tell anyone." Even though she and I knew that the first condition would not happen, the second condition would be kept because we had many little secrets together. Nevertheless, I promised her I would not ask questions or tell. Lucia grabbed her backpack and then told her mom, "We're going to the library because we have a lot of homework."

Like many times before, I thought we really were going there, but a few blocks later and knowing that the library was not in that direction, I finally asked, "What did you discover?" That's how fast I broke my first part of the promise, asking questions!

She opened the zipper of her backpack and showed me some bills. "Look, with this we can go buy candy, lots of candy! But we can't buy them close to our home because they know us and they're going to tell our moms!"

I started to taste the candy even before I bought it! We hopped on a bus and rode to a nearby town. When we got off and crossed the street, we ran to the candy store, where we bought all the candy that we could, remembering that we should save the money for a bus ticket to go home. While we waited for the bus, we sat on the sidewalk and began to remove the wrappers and eat them. Finally, after eating one of my favorite chocolates, I asked, "Where did you get the money?"

She rolled her eyes and answered, "I told you not to ask me! But hey, I'll tell you." (Ha ha ha, of course. If she did not tell me, then who?) "My mom has a lot of dollar bills in a jar, and I'm sure she does not know how much is in there. I had never realized, but this morning when I stayed at home I saw it, and I took a few. But don't worry, she won't notice!"

The worry came too late, because there would be no way to get the money back after having opened almost all of my candy. Once on the bus, we finished what we still had to eat, put all the wrappings in a bag, and threw them in the nearest trash can when we got out of the bus.

Before arriving at her mother's store, we checked each other to be sure there were no traces of candy on our faces, and we laughed at the thought that our stomachs would possibly hurt that night.

To our surprise, her mother was waiting for us! Addressing my friend, she asked her where the money was that she had taken. I did not know what to say. In my mind, the question of *"How did you know?"* was answered quickly. I realized we weren't as smart as we thought, because we'd forgotten that moms know everything!

Her mother, almost shouting, told us that she had to pay some bills that afternoon and went to her house to collect the money. (Of course she knew how much she had!) When she noticed that some money was missing, she went to look for us at the library, and when she didn't find us there, she knew we were buying candy (one of our little weaknesses). Lucia lowered her head at the loud scolding, because people in the store were witnessing the incident. Her mother made her extend her hands, and began to hit her with a leash.

I remembered the candy and chocolates that I had eaten and how I had enjoyed them, even the sour candies that were my friend's favorite. Unable to avoid it, I said, "It's my fault, too!" Lucia's mom looked at me, made us put our hands together, and hit us with the leash. She made us promise that we would never do it again. We responded in unison, "Never!"

My parents scolded me as well and told me that even though I had not taken the money, I was guilty because I had supported my friend and eaten the candy. I tried to explain that I did not know where she got the money until we had already bought the candy. They shook their heads when they told me, "If you had to hide, it was because you knew something was not right!" I looked at them and accepted that they were right. We had to repay that money by working odd jobs. As further punishment, we were forbidden from being together for two weeks. That was more painful than the work and the pain from our hands.

That experience made us realize that it is better not to do things that put us in trouble, especially when we know beforehand that we are not making good choices. It may be true that being friends makes us sisters because of everything that we lived through together. And just like sisters, we have to share the sweet, the sour, and—above all— the painfulness of any situation.

33

THE DECISION TO KNOW

The kitchen was full of girls ready to help, and we had planned an activity to have some money for our camp. Selling food was always a success, and we knew that it was not going to be different this time. Our families were the best customers because Mexican food was something that everyone liked.

My mother had a full-time job, and she didn't like to cook. I was at school every day, and nobody took the time to teach me to enjoy the magic of flavors and scents in the kitchen. Thus, my interest in this area was almost zero. I enjoyed being there, because I knew that something special was going to result after all the work. We were all chatting until the moment that somebody hit a spoon hard on a pot, trying to get our attention to give us our assignments.

I washed my hands before I started my chore. When I was ready, my friend had finished chopping the onion. I was fascinated to see how she used the knife; the small pieces looked like tiny squares measured with a ruler. When I complimented her, she laughed despite her tears. She handed me the knife and went to wash the cutting board while I took five big heads of lettuce out of a bag.

As I cut one in half, I heard a loud voice saying, "You don't know how to cut lettuce! Martha," she said, calling my friend's name, "you better do it! And you," she said, talking to me, "slice the tomatoes." I felt a little humiliated, but as soon as I saw the shredded lettuce in almost perfect strips, I knew for sure, who was going to slice the red and juicy tomatoes, and it was not me. In my eyes, my friend had an extraordinary ability. It's possible she had more experience, more dedication, or more love for the kitchen, and that is what made the difference.

A lot of time has passed since that day, and after all these years, I admit that when I realize that my food does not have the desired flavor or texture, I would like to give up, despite my interest in cooking. But that is when I remember the words of gratitude from the people I cook for. They know that sometimes the salt or the condiments are not adequate, but they always recognize my efforts, and they never forget to mention when I have cooked something delicious, and that inspires me to keep trying to improve.

I recognize that I don't have certain understanding or abilities. I still haven't developed perfection in every task or assignment; I can always improve if I follow the directions of people who have more knowledge in specific areas. I feel grateful to those who are willing to instruct me. On the other hand, when it is my time to teach, I remember how I felt many years ago when somebody didn't recognize my efforts in trying to help. I am still not perfect shredding lettuce, but I know that this doesn't qualify me as a bad cook. I'm not free of defects, but this doesn't mean that I am not a good person.

If somebody tells me, "You don't know!" I don't feel ashamed anymore. If that statement is true, it is an invitation to learn something that is reachable. It gives me motivation to immerse myself in a task, to gain a better insight into things that are new or to improve some aspects in my life. Nobody has all the answers, all the knowledge, or every skill perfected, but every step can bring us closer to certain perfection.

The answers to the questions how, why, and when are hidden truths that are waiting to be discovered. We just need to decide to find them and to enjoy the process of wanting *"to know."* But if we decide not to spend time or effort on learning, we must accept the consequences and finality of *"not knowing."*

34

THE LABEL

One morning when my alarm clock went off, I began to relate to cartoon characters that smash their alarm clocks with a hammer. I had only slept a couple of hours because I had stayed up all night writing a paper. On days like that, I regretted my decision to take college classes again. After so many years, my brain no longer worked the same, but my decision to learn English better and get a psychology degree motivated me to finish my assignments. I opened one eye, looking for the culprit of the repetitive sound that had awakened me. When I realized that it was my cell phone, I completely discarded the idea of destroying it.

As soon as I got up, I knew that it would be a complicated day. My to-do list was very long, and there was no option to postpone anything on the list. However, I took out a pen and with great satisfaction crossed off "psychology paper."

The hours ran together as I constantly checked off items on my list. At exactly two in the afternoon, I picked up my daughter to go to the college she was thinking of attending after high school graduation. We had an appointment with the counselor at three o'clock, so we stopped for a minute to buy lunch, since neither of us had time to eat before. The meeting lasted approximately one hour and fifteen minutes. When we left the counselor's office, we quickly went to buy a gift for my niece, whose birthday was the next day. We had already decided what to get her, so after only twenty minutes, we were on the road again.

We returned to the high school, where they were hosting a parent meeting to inform us about scholarships that our children could apply for. As I looked at the time on my cell phone, I smiled gratefully as I remembered the fleeting thought to destroy it that morning. I knew I had just over an hour left to spend at the parent meeting with my daughter. At exactly 6:25 I was running through the hallways to get to the parking lot. When I started my car, the clock read 6:28.

I had an appointment with my friend at 6:45 and then another at 7:00 in the same place. Fortunately, before leaving home that morning, I remembered that the possibility of going home to change after the parent meeting was low. For that reason, I had packed a navy blue dress, a pink sweater, a scarf, and shoes that would be appropriate for my plans in the evening.

Before opening the car door, I had already unzipped my pants. Since no one was around, I knew the car was the best place to change my clothes. I felt happy about the choice I had made, because I was ready in a couple of minutes. I arrived at my final destination for the evening and apologized to my friend for getting there a few minutes late; we enjoyed our conversation immensely for the next ten minutes.

When the time came, we went together to the venue. We planned to enjoy a program where a group of young women were exhibiting projects they had worked on to reach certain goals. Before entering, we were told that we would have fifteen minutes to go around and observe the girls' projects. My friend and I toured each table to greet many of the girls and asked them about the objects they were displaying. We finished our tour in the back, where I could finally admire the beautiful decorations that adorned the simple room.

While looking around, I recognized a beautiful woman whom I met three months ago. I knew that she was the one responsible for the decorations because she had a talent in transforming an ordinary place into something almost magical. I went to greet her, and I knew that she had seen me, but a few seconds later, she turned around and started walking the opposite direction. I was a little confused, but in that moment someone asked me a question and I momentarily forgot about the matter.

When I looked up, I saw the talented woman again, but now she marched toward me with scissors in hand. Without saying a word, she indicated that she was going to cut off the white laundry label that was hanging off my navy blue dress. I blushed from embarrassment as I realized that all this time I had been wearing my dress inside out. I quickly explained that I had changed in my car earlier that evening. My friend was very kind and understanding and assured me that "this was our secret." I thanked her, and although she told me no one else would notice, I went to the bathroom to fix my dress. When she saw me again, she smiled and—possibly without knowing it—made me feel very loved.

While enjoying the program that night, the thought came to me that I had never really paid attention to the laundering instruction label on my dress before. I had never followed the instructions that were indicated because I trusted my own experience. I imagine that we also have a label of care inside us, which we sometimes ignore because we believe that we do not need instructions. For example, the part that says that we should not be quick to judge is an important instruction to follow. I remembered the instantaneous feeling of sadness that I had when I thought my friend did not want to greet me. I felt rejected.

Hopefully we all have someone in our lives to help us "cut" what does not look good. Someone who can subtly approach us and tell us what is wrong and also is willing to keep it as "our secret." My dear friend's name in Hebrew means "she knew." I believe we should all adopt that meaning. Not only to "know" how to help someone in an embarrassing situation, but to "know" that it is necessary to read, remember, and follow the instructions on our inner label.

35

THE MAGICAL WORD

When my grandmother opened the door of her house, I could see her face light up with joy when she realized that my husband and I had dropped by to surprise her. The last time we had seen her was when we got married more than three years before. We greeted each other effusively and when she invited us to come in, the familiar smell of her cooking brought back many memories of my childhood. My parents, my brothers, and I had moved out of that city about twenty years ago, and even though we rarely visited her because of the long distance that separated us, our love for her was always present.

When we entered the kitchen, my grandma was ready to serve us food. I loved eating; however, the upset stomach that I had during the whole trip resurfaced. I explained to my grandmother that I had a stomachache and that as incredible as it seemed, I was not hungry. She approached me, took my face in her tiny hands, looked me straight in the eye, and said, "My girl, you're not sick—you're pregnant!"

I smiled sadly and explained to her that we had been to the doctor about a year before to try and find an answer to why we were having trouble getting pregnant. Again she looked at me and said, "I am certain. Certain like saying my name is Manuela. Soon a child will call you Mama!"

I looked at my grandmother with great love, hugged her, and only dared to say, "I wish it were so."

Oliver, our first child, was born seven months after the day we visited my beloved grandmother. How did she know? When I asked her, her answer was, "I only knew, and that's it." When I heard her, I knew that she would not give me more explanation, because that had always been her answer when someone asked how she knew things in advance.

Our son started talking when he was about one year old; he learned to say *dad, water, kiss, goodbye,* and *Rosie.* For more than eleven months, I sat in front of him and explained that I was Mom. I invited him to repeat the word after me when I pointed to myself: "Mommy, Mommy!" He would laugh and repeat after me, but as soon as he needed me, he would call me, "Rosie!" I couldn't understand how a child so young could roll his R's so perfectly to call my name instead of simply calling me mom, which in my mind required less effort.

When he turned two, he received some toys to play with in the garden, so a few days after his birthday he asked me to let him play outside. I had many things to do that morning, but I could watch him through the kitchen window. Seeing him run with the ball, I marveled that this child was my son, although I still had not been able to make him understand that I was not Rosie, I was Mom. This happened because my husband, brothers, parents, and friends always referred to me by name. Nobody called me mom.

I was not surprised that afternoon when, after spending some time running into the kitchen, he said, "Rosie, I want water, please!" When he finished drinking the water, he gave me the glass and returned to the backyard. I peeked out the window to be sure he was okay, but then for a few minutes I only listened to him. I knew he could still entertain himself. Several times he would shout my name so that I would see him do a somersault on the lawn or run and jump.

When I heard my name once more a few minutes later, I thought he wanted to show me something he was doing, so I told him in a loud voice that in a minute I was going to see him, because I was finishing cleaning his bedroom. Twice more I heard him say, "Rosie, Rosie!" I went slowly to the kitchen window, but when I heard him scream, "Mommy, Mommy, help me!" I knew something strange was happening, and I ran into the yard.

When I saw my son hanging from the top of a high fence that divided our house from the neighbor's, the first thing I did was to run and take him in my arms; I hugged him and let him know that he was safe. He had set up a small table, chair, and box as if they were a ladder to help him see the puppy that had been barking in our neighbor's garden. With his hands on the edge, he had unintentionally kicked the chair and knocked down the box with it. After I held him in my arms for a few moments, I felt grateful that he had not hurt himself, and I blamed myself for not paying enough attention to him.

When I put him on the floor, I hugged him tightly again and started crying when he said, "Thank you, Mommy, I love you so much." That night, I called my grandmother to tell her that the second part of what she had told me would happen was finally a reality, because since the incident in the garden that morning, Oliver did not call me again by my name. Now I was "Mommy"—a word that sounds magical to me.

Over the years, it still seems incredible to me that not just one person but four call me mom. I feel happy when my son or three daughters do not hesitate to use the magic word when they need my help, my advice, or simply to share their joys or challenges. This word inspires me to run by their side and enjoy the blessing that I am able to share my life with them. I love embracing them and making them feel my love.

My suggestions are not always the most accurate or the wisest, but they are at that moment in my understanding the ones that are the best. But if they make a decision that is different from the one I recommended and things do not go well, I do not blame them, because I know that it is part of their own learning. When their decision was better than the one I proposed, I let them know that just because I'm older doesn't mean I'm smarter. I do not intend for them to stop discovering what is beyond our own home. I do not think that they are safe only by my side and even though I feel that on many occasions I could have paid more attention to protect them, I know that I cannot always prevent painful moments in their lives.

Many times, when I feel that I am about to fall and hurt myself by some difficult situation that I face in my own life, I do not hesitate to pick up the phone and say the magical word, "Mommy," to the woman who is always willing to extend her help and love or to give me her opinion. How do I know that she is always there for me? I can respond as my grandmother did: "I only know, and that's enough." I hope that my own children can have that same knowledge as well.

36

THE OLD AND THE WISE

My first encounter with the wisdom of an older person came one day when I entered my Logic class and I saw countless sheets ranging from the brightest white to a really dark gray. My teacher explained that everything is a matter of perspective; white can be black and black can be white. I inspected each sheet and noticed that between one color and another there was really almost no difference if their tones were close enough. As I moved from the light to the dark, I marveled to discover that almost imperceptibly, the white ceased to be after many changes of tone.

At fifteen years old, I began to feel great admiration for those who taught lessons that inspired me to learn more about everything that surrounded me. I do not know how old my teacher was, but in my eyes, he was very old because his hair and wrinkles portrayed the passage of time. That was the day when I began to associate wisdom with age.

A couple years later, I confirmed what I had learned once again. This time, I was enrolled in a nutrition class. Upon first looking at my teacher, I knew that she was a person who understood the world in a way that was still unknown to me. Not only did her knowledge tell me her age, but her style of clothes did as well.

I never imagined that one day someone would tell me that I was an older person, because at eighteen, the wrinkles had not yet appeared on my face. So I was surprised for a moment when I was teaching a class of children. While asking them their names and ages, most children responded that they were three years old. However, one girl with arrogance announced, "I'm not three, I'm four years old. I'm older than all of them." I smiled, knowing that for her, being older somehow put her in a different situation where I should show her more respect.

I told them my name and asked them how old they thought I was. Everyone looked at me closely, and I heard a voice saying, "Like a hundred years old?" For a moment I expected to hear some laughter, letting me know that they were joking, but all I saw were little faces nodding, or believing that was true. When I told them I was only eighteen, the older girl looked surprised and said, "Wow! Those are sooooo many years. You're so old!" Fortunately, there was not another adult around who could agree with that comment, so I continued with my class.

That afternoon when I got home, I remembered the children's comments and, out of sheer curiosity, I went to the mirror in the bathroom and checked my face to be sure I did not have any lines of expression. As a precaution, I put a larger than normal amount of cream on my face and neck. I looked at myself and concluded that what they had seen in me was just a person with more knowledge.

Twenty years later, I was talking to a group of women over fifty-five about how important it is to recognize that being happy is a personal decision and that no one can make that decision for us no matter how hard they try. At the end of my presentation as I was saying goodbye, one lady took me by the arm and told one of her classmates, "I love this girl. She reminds me of when I was her age, when I saw things differently." Both women smiled and thanked me for being there.

When I got into my car, the first thing I did was lower the mirror, and I looked at myself carefully once again. For a moment, I thought that I should not have agreed to speak in front of a group of people with more experience and that my knowledge was not enough to share the desire to look for reasons in each stage of life to smile and enjoy the journey. Then I remembered that day when some children called me an old woman, and compared that to now when I examined myself again in a mirror. My conclusion was that I had been called a girl, not because of my lack of wisdom, but because my wrinkles were less than theirs and my gray hair had been covered with hair dye just a few days before.

At eighteen, the children considered me to be old, while I considered myself to be wise. At thirty-eight, someone surely believed that I did not have the wisdom to give advice. She did not mention being a girl in relation to being young, but rather to lack of experience. In the end, however, the most important thing is what the mirror makes me believe, or what I make the mirror believe, because opinions vary from person to person. If I ask a twenty-year-old if I am old and have wisdom, he or she will most likely say yes. But if I ask someone of eighty years if I am old and experienced in this life, he or she will tell me that I have not lived enough years yet.

Years and wisdom do not necessarily go hand in hand and although they could be disguised, they cannot be hidden. The answer to whether we are old and hopefully wise is a matter of perspective. It is better to look at ourselves in the mirror, not to know how we look, but to confirm that we are what we want to see.

37

THE SLOWEST TURTLE

"How much does that turtle cost?" Abad asked the shopkeeper in the small gift shop that was near our high school.

Upon hearing the price, I said, "Wow! Hey, that's a lot!"

"Yes, but it's worth it," she replied.

I loved visiting the small gift shop, because the stuffed animals that were sold there were very nice. In addition, one could ask the shop owners to hold a toy for you while you made small payments until you finally owned it. In those years, giving or receiving one of those stuffed animals was very special. I enjoyed the times in the small gift shop where I could admire those little treasures.

Abad and I met by pure chance. She was in a different class from mine, and she attended school in the afternoon, while I attended in the morning. When I saw her for the first time, it surprised me. The school hour was over and my classmates and I went to a café where we could have a soda and listen to music. Those were the moments when we talked about everything and everyone. Plus, there was a small microphone where any brave person could sing, even if they didn't have a good voice. That day we were applauding and encouraging our friend who had decided that one day she wanted to be a singer. We predicted that she would not have much success, even though we loved her and admired her courage.

Abad approached me and asked, "Hey, aside from reciting poetry, do you like music?" As I turned around to answer her, I realized she was missing an eye. Never before had I seen someone without an eye! I tried not to stare, but it was one of those situations where you do not know what to do or how to act. However, with a big smile that showed off incredibly perfect teeth, Abad said, "I look at you with this eye because it's the only one I have, but you have no excuse not to look at me with both of your eyes!" At that moment, a friendship was born.

She told me that she had heard me in a poetry contest at school, and that she did not like to recite poetry, but she loved to write it and collect it from other authors. She promised that she would bring me some that were her favorites so that I could read them and if I liked them, she would share them with me. For the next few weeks, we met at the café before I began classes. We talked about what type of poems we liked to read and what music we liked to hear. Fortunately, she had the chance to change her schedule and start school at the same time that I did, so we were able to spend more time together.

Few people felt comfortable around Abad, but she didn't mind. One day she recounted the story of how she lost her eye in an accident some years before. She was playing with a stick in her backyard and lost her balance. I asked her if it was hard to live with only one eye. "I see the same as others," she replied. "The problem is that others do not see me the same."

We all have certain skills and abilities; for Abad it was running. She was a very talented runner; not only did she have great physical abilities, but she was very fast, earning many medals in a variety of sports. On the other hand, I always came last … well, possibly with a couple of exceptions. On one occasion, I said, "If members from my volleyball team were like you with that great speed and condition, we would be the best team." She gave me a nice smile and said, "If I could see and talk like you, I would be the best at reciting poetry and playing volleyball, because then the ball would not hit me so often." Her words made me understand that we cannot complain about what we don't have; we must learn to enjoy what we do have.

As time passed and our friendship grew, I realized that Abad and I were not that different after all. For me, and for all of us who had the opportunity to really know her, she was simply one of us. Just like the rest of us, Abad dreamed about her future, complained about what she did not like, and enjoyed her achievements. When we told her that she always saw life with rose-colored glasses, she made us laugh when she said, "I do not see life like that. Life is painted that color because it's my favorite!" We all loved our friend Abad because she helped us see more than what we were capable of seeing with two eyes.

Sadly, my dear friend moved away before the end of the school year. Before leaving she gave me a gift, a stuffed animal with a very special note that said, "For the slowest turtle I have ever known, but with who it has been worth walking through this life."

To this day, turtles remind me that our situations, our abilities, and the colors we see life through might be different, but we will always find people who are worth walking through this life by their side.

38

TRUSTING IN MORE THAN OUR OWN DECISIONS

When reviewing brochures of different universities with my daughter, I realized that many times it's not so easy to make decisions that affect the rest of our life. Many options to achieve certain goals often make us afraid to make a mistake. On one occasion, my daughter asked my husband and me where we would like her to go to college. Our response was quick and without hesitation: "We want you to go to the place that *you* like."

Our daughter has always liked to study and get good grades. We remember a certain day when she was in third grade, because she was very worried after obtaining a grade that, according to her, could affect her grade point average in such a way that it could eliminate her chances of going to college. We explained that we were very happy that she always tried to learn, but that there was still a long time for that moment to come.

The years passed, and we had the opportunity to visit some colleges with her. Even when each one seemed to fulfill her aspirations, it was not yet clear which was her first option. As the day to send applications got closer and closer, the pressure was greater, and a decision had to be made. The door of her bedroom remained closed many evenings while she concentrated on applying for scholarships.

One of those evenings after opening her door to cheer her up, she asked if I had a few minutes. I sat next to her right then and she asked me, "Mom, how did you decide to go to the school where you studied? Was that where you wanted to go? Was it an easy choice for you?"

It had been a long time since those days, so it took me a few moments to remember, and then I shared my story with her.

From fifteen- to eighteen-years-old I had had the opportunity to study at a private school in Mexico City. All my life, I had lived in small towns far from the big cities, so the change had been incredible for me. During that time, I knew that I would study at the most emblematic university in the country—the National Autonomous University of Mexico. When I was almost finished with my third year of high school, I told my parents my decision. That day, I saw a lot of sadness in their faces as they told me that it was not so easy, because they did not have the money for me to continue living in Mexico City and at the same time help me pay for school. My dad, at that moment, had an idea: he would ask a family we had met if I could live with them, because they knew that their only daughter would get married very soon and would no longer live with them.

A few weeks later, I received the answer I longed for. Yes, the answer was yes. The apartment where that family lived was very small. They had three children—the oldest used a closet they had made into a bedroom, and the two younger boys shared a very small bedroom. The daughter who was getting married would move in July, so I could start living there in August. Everything was falling into place perfectly.

The time came for me to take the admission exam even though I was full of nervous butterflies, but I kept confident that everything would be fine. I had been taught that I could ask for help from our Heavenly Father at any time, and with my own efforts and His help, the correct answers always arrived. I had no doubt that this would be the case during the test. When I received the notification that I had been accepted to my dream university, I felt very happy and began to plan and visualize what my life would be like from then on.

My happiness was short-lived. When I was back home after finishing high school in July, we received the news that I could not live where I had planned, because the girl had decided not to get married. I had no other choice, so after crying and mentally unpacking my bags, I knew that I should apply to the university near my home. I was accepted, and that was the reason I chose it.

When I finished telling that story to my daughter, I explained that what she had now was a blessing that I did not have at that time. She could actually decide where she wanted to go. I asked her to depend on our Heavenly Father as well, because He would undoubtedly help her feel what would be the best decision. We hugged, and when I was about to leave her room, she asked me, "Do you still feel sad because you did not have the opportunity to go to the school of your dreams?" I smiled and said no, because if it had worked out as I planned, the chances that I would have married her father would have been almost zero, and then we would not be having this conversation. We both laughed again.

A moment later, she asked me something that had never crossed my mind. "Mommy, are your parents still friends with that family?" And in answering, "No, we never saw them again," the thoughts crowded in my mind in such a way that I realized that for more than thirty years, I had never thought about what could have been and never was.

Surprise and sadness took over at the same time. My daughter thought she had said something wrong, and between sobs, I told her what I had discovered at that moment.

It was the year 1985 when I finished high school. If everything had happened as I had planned it, in the month of August I would have started living in Mexico City. We never heard from that family again, simply because on September 19, 1985, there was a big earthquake in Mexico City that brought down the apartment building where they lived; the only one that survived was the youngest of the children; the school bus had picked him up before seven in the morning.

Approximately ten thousand people lost their lives in the earthquake. That day, I was running with a group of friends on a beach in another part of the country.

My daughter hugged me, cried next to me, and told me that from that moment on, she would not only trust in her own choices, but she would ask for the guidance of our Heavenly Father to know and feel that those were the best decisions for her life.

Incredible as it may seem, I never stopped to think about why things did not turn out the way had I wanted them to. I just continued with my life and found other options that would make me happy. The only thing I regret is that I did not realize that blessing sooner.

I know that many times when we set goals and follow a path to reach them, we feel frustrated when, after having worked so hard, the results are not what we wanted. We may have come to think that there is something or someone who is opposed to us reaching what we think would give us great satisfaction. If we have given our best effort and depended on the right help, we should not feel afraid to make mistakes.

Even though on many occasions what we have obtained is different than what we desired, those things we have received will be the best for our lives, even if it takes some time to recognize it.

39

UNNECESSARY RISKS

It was eleven o'clock at night when we left the party. My group of friends and I started walking outside the room where there were activities to raise funds to help schools every week. Fridays were our favorite days because we always found a way to have fun and spend time together. We were very happy to belong to that group of friends.

It was not easy to get permission to go to such events, because our parents always reminded us that even if we lived in a small town, we should always take precautions and look out for each other. That night was no exception—the rule was that we should be home no later than midnight. But at a party like this, leaving at midnight was like leaving the party when it was just starting.

In my case, the situation was a bit different because, at that age, my parents lived in another country, and I lived alone with my three younger brothers. Incredible as it seems, I followed the same rules as my friends, because for many years, my parents' advice had been the same. Also, every week when I talked on the phone with them, they asked me for a report of what we had experienced during the week. My brothers were not interested in these kinds of activities, so they usually stayed home. When I returned home, they were almost always asleep.

That night, my friends and I decided to stop at a sandwich shop because we were all hungry. We realized that while we were at the party, a torrential rain had fallen. The streets looked less busy than usual. None of us had a car, so we always had to walk, which was a delight before we had to separate for a few blocks to get to our respective homes. Looking at my watch, I realized that it was almost midnight, and I told them we should hurry. Everyone started to laugh and told me that I should be the least worried since my parents were not even in the country.

When we left the sandwich shop, we could still hear the music from a distance, and someone commented that he thought there was no difference between going home at midnight or two hours later. As we continued our journey, we suddenly realized that there were many dead birds on the street. There is always someone who has an explanation for everything, so we stopped, and eight of us turned our heads toward the wise one of our group. He pointed to the large tree on the side of the street. During the night, it was difficult to make out, because its huge branches were full of leaves. At that time it was easy to confuse it with darkness. But we were all familiar with the tree, because many times we had used it as a point of reference.

Rafael explained that this tree was the home of many birds, and we nodded, because every day we heard birds singing. He continued, saying that for years he had observed many nests in the tree, so there were always mother birds waiting for their children to break through their shells. The birds lived there because the tree gave them protection from the other animals and also from the inclement weather, but this time, the hail that fell was so big that it killed many of the birds.

Possibly to break the moment of discomfort from learning what happened to the birds, somebody said, "They really had bad luck." Another boy from my group commented, "You see, they were home and could not save themselves, which means that we can get hurt wherever we are. I am sure now that it would not be such a bad idea to return to the party."

Again Rafael gave his opinion: "You are right, these birds died practically while asleep—but not because they were exposed without reason. I am sure that what happened today is not common, because if it were, the adults would look for another way to protect their young and survive themselves." We did not need more motivation to start walking toward the protection of our homes. We all agreed that it is unnecessary to take risks that can put us in greater danger.

My friends and I learned a great lesson. There is always a chance that something unfortunate can happen to us while at home, but the odds are less when we follow the advice of those who have more experience and who know how to protect the nests where we grow up. We all take risks no matter where we are, but some risks are unnecessary. If we make the best decision, our safety increases. Of course, there are situations that we cannot control—it is what one of our friends called "bad luck"—but taking precautions and making good decisions are always under our control.

40

UNTIL OUR LAST BREATH

When I was seven years old, I heard a neighbor frantically tell my mom that the world would end in the year 1982. At that time, I was learning to add in school, so I realized that I would not live to celebrate my fifteenth birthday. However, I didn't feel too sad about the news, because at the age of seven, eight years seemed like a lifetime. In my house, as in many others, there was a rule that children do not listen to adult conversations. To avoid a scolding from my mother, I did not comment on what I had heard and what I thought I knew.

As the months passed, I forgot about the conversation, and like a typical child, I dedicated myself to enjoy every moment. At that time, the days seemed long, which gave me the opportunity to go to school, play, read, do homework, watch television, and share responsibilities with my siblings at home. It never crossed my mind that the day lacked the hours to carry out all these activities. At night I do not remember waking up for any reason, except for going to the bathroom. The word "sleepless" was not in my vocabulary.

Upon returning to school after the holiday break in December, the teacher reminded us that it was a different year and that we should write it down at the top of our notebook pages each time we took notes. I was horrified, knowing that now there were only seven years left until the world ended. However, after my fright passed, I didn't think for another second about only having seven years left on Earth.

I never doubted that what I had heard as a curious seven-year-old wasn't true, because when my mom and her friends said that someone was going to have a baby in a few months, the baby appeared. If they mentioned that someone would move, after a while we stopped seeing them. Furthermore, when they told me that the measles would disappear if I did not scratch, that's exactly what happened, just like when my teeth fell out, and they said that new ones would grow. How could I doubt them when everything they had ever told me came true?

A year later, I again remembered about the big event coming up when I wrote down the new year in my notebook. Now there were only six years left until the world would end! Keeping that in mind, when one of my aunts asked me what I would like to be when I grew up, I answered that it didn't matter because I was going to die before I turned fifteen. My mother heard my reply and asked me why I was so sure that I wouldn't live to be fifteen years old. Unable to hide it any longer, I admitted that I had eavesdropped on a certain conversation a couple years ago.

My mom hugged me and assured me that I should not worry, because when she was my age, everyone said that there would be a flood that would swallow the earth. She continued that ever since she heard that rumor, she had only witnessed mild rainstorms.

I asked her, "But do you think it will happen?"

"I do not know," was her honest response, "but I'm not going to waste my life with that kind of fear. You have to learn that life on this Earth doesn't end until you stop breathing. What you should worry about is doing good things in this life if you want to live in heaven after."

I remembered her words again when I was in a store towards the end of the year 1999, when everything was in utter chaos, because in a few days the checks we wrote would carry the year 2000. However, no one was sure if we would make it to that year. Fortunately, as in the days of my childhood, everyone's fear was short-lived. Over the next few days, months, and years, everyone's fear dissipated. Although now my knowledge and my years on this earth are greater and the hours of each one of my days seem not to be enough, I still believe my mom's words. Since I am still breathing, my biggest concern is trying to do things well, because I hope to live in a better place after this life.

41

WHERE DO I WANT TO GO?

D erek, a small seeker of innate adventures, had come to his family as the awaited male after the birth of his two beautiful sisters, Taylor and Jordan. They were two very intelligent girls and really intrepid. They were an inspiration to their brother, who tried to match them in the risks they took. The girls applauded each of his conquests and when trying to emerge victorious from some mischief and when he got hurt, they were not only there to give him comfort but also to encourage him, letting him know that the next time he could do it, or if not, it would hurt less.

There were always laughter and jokes among the siblings. Taylor always tried to act more mature, knowing that she was the oldest; she thought that she should be a good example, but at playtime she would forget. Jordan frequently showed marks of her bravery, such as the day she received twelve stitches on her head for trying to jump too high, or when she appeared with raccoon eyes because a door fell on her.

One day, Derek discovered that he fit in the space between the two front doors. The first door was a screen door that could only be opened from the inside. It was used it to let the air enter the house on warm days, and it prevented flies from coming into the house. The door behind that was like any regular door that was locked when the family went out. The boy realized that if he stood on his tiptoes and raised his arms, there was enough space for his little body. My son Oliver helped him complete the challenge his sisters were too big to accomplish. Oliver, who was a year older, closed the first door, and when Derek settled in, Oliver pushed the second door closed and locked it.

The two were very happy to have achieved their goal. Finally, someone had been caught between the two doors. When we heard their cries of joy while we were unloading grocery bags from the car, the girls and I laughed after seeing what they had done.

The joy did not last long, though, because when Derek wanted to get out of the tight spot he was in, we realized that the keys were inside the house. The first door was out of our reach to open, and the second door was locked. I turned around, trying to enter through the back door, but that one was also locked. When I heard Derek begin to sob, his sisters jumped into action. "Derek, open the door!" they said to him through the screen door that only opened from the inside. The boy could barely reach the knobs, but even with his back to one of the doors, he could move his hands to try to unlock either of them. He broke down in tears and between babbling answered, "Which door?"

"Whichever!" I heard them say.

We heard his trembling voice saying, "I just do not know where I want to go!" The girls looked at me, rolling their eyes, and then Taylor said, "Open the door you want, jump out of there, and then decide if you want go inside the house or outside."

Finally, and with great effort, Derek stood on his tiptoes, reached for the knob in front of him, unlocked it, and ran to us. We all embraced him and expressed our admiration for his bravery for getting out of a tight spot. A few moments later, I saw him running, shouting, and laughing all over the house, already forgetting the incident from a few moments before.

How many times have I felt imprisoned between two doors simply because I did not know where I wanted to go? Many times! I often feel trapped until I make the decision to raise my hands to free myself from a situation that is not pleasant, but that I put myself into. Sometimes I even receive a little help from others.

Even if someone else tries to get me out of the problem and puts all their encouragement into the help, it cannot be achieved if I do not make the decision. Where do I want to go? That's the question we must answer when we feel that we are losing our freedom by making wrong choices. If we have doubts about which is our best destination, the most important thing is to remember the words of a couple girls who knew: "Open the door you want, jump out of there, and then decide where you want to go!"

When we feel free again, we will see more clearly which is the best path to follow!

42

WITH ROUGH SOLES

It was nine in the morning, and we were at the bus terminal, ready to enjoy the beginning of summer. My group of friends, ages ranging between sixteen and twenty-one years old, always found a way to enjoy our time together. Lack of money was never an impediment for us to plan and live adventures that we would cherish forever. About twenty of us shared not only the desire to have fun, but to learn, to support, and to serve.

That morning we had decided to swim at a water canal that was in a town thirty minutes from where most of us lived. We were certain we would have a great day. When we saw the bus that would take us to our destination, we ran to get in. We wanted to be the first to board so we could claim all the seats in the back. We did not wait for anyone else, because if someone decided to join the adventure later, they would certainly know where to find us.

The bus stopped at least eight places on its route through the small towns before finally arriving at our destination. With backpacks and bags in hand, we walked through the dusty streets until we reached the place most of us had previously visited. Without wasting time, we looked for the perfect spot to drop off our belongings and start swimming. There were no trees around, no sunscreen, and no table to place the sandwiches in our bags. The only plan we had was to be there—the rest was not important.

One by one we started to jump into the canal. We swam against the current until it dragged us a few meters back, and then we jumped out so we did not have to walk so far back to the spot where we began. The soles of our feet began to develop calluses because the canal was made of cement. To get out of it, we had to climb the rough sides; in addition, we walked on the ground for a few meters to jump off our designated spot. However, without a doubt, none of us cared.

An hour later, I realized that a girl I did not know had arrived. She was the niece of one of my friends. As always, the boys, seeing someone new, were willing to show off their chivalry. That always caused us to laugh, because we knew that if she continued to frequent our group, in a couple of weeks, they would forget trying to impress Miriam.

After the presentations of bravery from the boys in the canal, she, like everyone else, took off the clothes she was wearing over her swimsuit. I forgot about her for a few moments, until I realized that she had not swum in the canal yet. I asked her if she was going to swim, and she said, "Yes, in a few minutes."

It was time to eat, and we all looked for rocks to sit on because we never brought chairs. From our backpacks came all kinds of food, such as bread, sandwiches, fruit, and sweets. We all shared the food we brought. No one was left without food, even if there was nothing in our house to bring. That was what brought us closer. There were never uncomfortable questions, nor envies, nor complaints. All the moments we shared were full of joy.

Within a few minutes, we were ready to return to the water. I do not know how many times someone told us that we should wait for our food to digest before swimming, but being young, we threw this advice to the wind and went back quickly to the water. I heard someone ask Miriam if she was going to swim in the canal, she again answered, "Yes, in a little while." In a few minutes, someone again urged her to get in the water, and one of the boys swimming in the canal shouted, "What, do you not know how to swim?!"

She immediately answered, "Of course I do!"

Knowing we would have to leave soon, a small group of us ventured to go a little farther down the canal, so that when we returned to our spot we would be in dry bathing suits. It took us a few minutes to return, and when we were back with the whole group, someone suggested that we stay another thirty minutes. I thought I would not get wet again, so I decided to sit by Miriam next to the canal. I asked her if she had decided not to swim because she was on her period. She smiled and told me no, and once again said that in a moment she would get in. At that precise moment, someone came to push me into the water. That was part of our games; one had to be careful when they were dry, because there would always be someone who tried to get us all wet again. In trying to resist, I took Miriam by the arm, and they pushed us both in.

When immersed in the water, I was grateful to be there, because the water was more than refreshing on that hot day. As soon as I stuck my head out, I heard screams that I did not understand. Finally, I paid attention and realized that the current was dragging my friend's niece. Someone ran to help her and although the anguish lasted only a few seconds, we all managed to get her out.

There was a great silence; we had never had that experience before. Then I heard a voice addressing me, saying, "Because of you, I almost drowned!"

I looked at her, my face full of astonishment, and the only thing that came out of my mouth was, "Meeeeee?"

Miriam nodded.

I felt all eyes on me, almost accusing me, and without thinking twice I said, "I had no plan to get wet again and even less to push you. But if you were going to drown, it was going to be your own fault for not admitting that you don't know how to swim. We all asked you and you never admitted it!"

I got out of the canal and put on my clothes. While gathering my things, I heard someone say about Miriam, "I knew she couldn't swim because her feet look smooth and not rough!" Unable to avoid it, I laughed. I gathered my things and started walking toward the road where the bus would pass to take me back home.

As I had to wait for the next bus, everyone caught up with me, and together we went back home. No one commented about the incident, but the jokes and laughter returned as if nothing unusual had happened. As we said goodbye, one of the girls said about Miriam, "I think her feet are rough anyway, even if she doesn't swim!" Of course, we all laughed. Miriam eventually learned how to swim, and for many years we continued to enjoy our adventures.

We need to remember that a characteristic such as having rough soles is not an indication of any ability. We cannot assume that someone knows or does not know about something because of the way they look. On the other hand, it is not necessary to say we know something we haven't learned just to keep from feeling out of place, because in the long run, we may have to demonstrate that knowledge we claim is ours.

As with the majority of the people, when somebody is lying to me, I feel disappointed, and think that I cannot trust them anymore. But when I remember that sometimes we lie or shade the truth because we are afraid to be sincere, fearing rejection and judgment, even for simple mistakes, I am ready to forgive. I am ready to free myself of negative emotions. I am ready to accept my own responsibility, because many times I question myself. People often lie because they don't trust that my reaction to the truth is going to be one of acceptance. I am ready to have joy, to be kind, to laugh again, and to ask myself for forgiveness when I make my own mistakes.

43

WITHOUT AN INVITATION

"Happy birthday!" I told the owner of the house, giving her a small gift. I purposely said it without saying her name, because if I was being totally honest, I did not remember it.

That afternoon, Claudia and I had planned to go out together, but unexpectedly I received a call saying that the plans had changed, "Do you remember the woman who went bowling with us and lived in Germany many years ago?"

"No, I don't remember," I replied.

"Well, it doesn't matter. She invited us to her house tonight because it's her birthday, and I think we'll have a great time. When you see her, I'm sure you'll recognize her!"

I was not excited to attend a birthday party where I did not know who we were celebrating, but when my friend explained that the birthday woman had agreed to let me come, it did not seem inconvenient to go somewhere else while still being with my good friend.

Without further questions, I wrote down the address. I stopped in a store first to buy a gift that did not take me a long time to choose because I did not know the birthday lady's taste or her age or even her name. I opted for something that any woman would be pleased with: a gift card for a spa.

Arriving at the address, I rang the doorbell with the confidence that people were waiting for me to show up. However, when I stepped inside, I noticed a small group of women who seemed to know each other very well. I felt uncomfortable not knowing whose birthday party it was or who to give the gift to! The feeling was only momentary, because I finally saw a face that smiled at me when she said, "Good thing you came!" At that moment, I knew that the night was going to be fun. Claudia and I have the joy of knowing each other since we were teenagers. We had enjoyed many evenings together and shared a thousand stories, so every time we see each other or talk, we enjoy every moment.

After greeting us, the owner of the house approached us, and I delivered the gift and congratulated her. Then the introductions were made: "You remember Alejandra, right?" *No,* I thought, but knowing that I was expected to say yes, I said, "Yes, of course!" And then we started talking about the day when "we met."

We sat around the table, eating a delicious dinner, and I realized that the hostess enjoyed making her guests feel good. We talked about everything and possibly nothing in particular, that's how fast time went by, and when I discovered that the midnight had arrived, I knew it was time to say goodbye after having enjoyed a lovely party. I said goodbye to my friend, and Alejandra walked me to the door. We agreed that it would be great to see each other again.

On my way home, I smiled to myself. It had been one of those magical evenings where you are so comfortable that time is the least important thing on your mind.

A couple of weeks later, I saw Alejandra again. We enjoyed our conversation and over time, we admitted that we did not remember meeting each other before that moment on her birthday. In fact, when I entered her home, she had asked one of her friends, "Who invited her?"

Though many years have passed by, Alejandra and I have been present at each other's special moments for our families. There is no celebration in our home without her being included; there are no sorrows that have ceased to be shared. Our children, even if they were born in different parts of the world and have learned to say their first words in a different language, have discovered that we can choose who we call family.

When our children began to marry, it never seemed strange to us that a newcomer would become part of our families so quickly. We understand that there are few people you have the opportunity to share your complete thoughts with. In these thoughts there are questions, answers, opinions, and reasoning that are not expressed for fear of hurting, creating tension, or simply because one believes that it is not the right time. Realizing that you can expose yourself without fear of being judged or misinterpreted, you know you have found one of your other selves, and most of the time you found them without planning to.

When you realize that the need to talk to yourself is less frequent, it is because many times, without thinking or searching, you have found someone to talk with. Your spouse or friend may have been completely unknown until they suddenly appeared in your life and became an essential part of it, because you opened the door to that opportunity.

We must appreciate the presence of those who arrive unexpectedly in our lives. We never know in advance who will share our greatest moments of happiness or sadness, especially when that person comes into our lives without an invitation.

44

WITHOUT GUESSING

"I know you're going to be fine!" were the last words I heard from my mother that Sunday when she left me in that new school.

We had traveled by bus about three hours to get there. The decision had been made months in advance, and although I doubted a thousand times that this was what I wanted to do, I knew from all the explanations I had been given that this was the best school for me at that time. The opportunity to attend a prestigious boarding school was not easy to refuse.

At only fifteen years of age, all sound reasoning stopped being valid the moment I saw my mother say goodbye and walk away. I wanted to run to her and ask her not to leave me there, but I prevented the urge to run because I knew that around me were other girls who were also saying goodbye to their parents. However, in my eyes, they not only looked calm, but happy.

I returned to the house where I would spend the next school year. My feet felt unusually heavy that day when I walked, and I felt that I was drowning! There was a strange tightness in my chest; someone later described it to me as uncertainty, the fear of not knowing what will happen next.

I went to the bedroom that I would share with three other girls. I had been there with my mom a couple of hours before, and we had moved my few belongings into my assigned closet. It was a room with two bunk beds, a table, four chairs, and a connected bathroom. Through the single window, we had a view of the backyard that offered no inspiration.

To my surprise, one of the girls was already settling in, too. "What's your name?" she asked me, and without giving me time to answer, she continued, "I am Claudia, and I hope you don't mind sleeping on the bottom bunk, because I already claimed the top." I looked at the beds for a few seconds and thought that I wanted to be in the only place where I felt safe at that age: my own house! Before I could explain that I didn't mind the bottom bunk, she began placing some things on the bed she had chosen, and continued her monologue. "Hopefully, the other two girls who are going to stay here are fun and do not cause many problems."

I thought, *And hopefully they don't talk as much.*

Generally, I was the most talkative person in any conversation. But on that occasion, I felt really uncomfortable in a place completely unknown to me, where everything was new: the city, the place I would call home, and the people that I had never seen until that moment. The only woman I wanted to be with and with whom I felt safe since I had arrived had already left.

Suddenly, I realized that my roommate was waiting for me near the door. I was so immersed in my own thoughts that I had lost part of her conversation, but she did not seem to notice, because I heard her say, "In spite of everything, the summer was very long; I couldn't wait to return to school!" Then I understood that she had attended the year before. Seeing her so happy and carefree, I thought that my time in this school would not be so difficult. With a laugh she warned me, "I hope you're ready to eat the dish that distinguishes this place," and again without waiting for my comment, she headed to the dining room while I followed.

I think I had no interest in what was happening since I had arrived, because ten girls were already sitting around the table, while I had only seen two before.

I laughed to discover that what I heard about dinner was true! What we ate that night was something I had never tasted before, and it would be the most repeated menu item for the next three years while I lived in that beautiful place. They call them "molletes," which is white bread cut in half, covered with beans and cheese that melts when put in the oven and makes them crispy. The recipe sounds simple and bland, but they are really delicious.

When the time came to go to bed, and our other roommates had arrived, I imagined they were just as overwhelmed as I was, because they didn't talk too much either. That night, the moment my head touched the pillow, it was not tiredness that made my eyes close, but the tears that came outside of my control. I expected no one could hear me and I think that probably was the case, because I listened to the slow breathing of someone in the bed above and the movements of two people trying to silence their own sobs across the room.

The next morning when I was ready to go to breakfast, I realized that I had forgotten to bring something very important from my house. I didn't actually forget it, because it was something that I never thought I was going to use in a school where a uniform was not required: long socks! I knew that the dress code was to wear dresses every day, but long socks? When I saw my roommates put their socks on, I did not worry too much until I arrived at the dining room and noticed that the only one not wearing long socks was me.

As we sat around the table, Claudia slipped a pair of socks in my lap, and in a whisper and calling me by name told me, "In this place, sadness and joy are not the only things that are shared. Everything that we have is available when someone else needs it." I imagine that she knew that I was that someone, since she saw that my closet was so small and still had enough space to accommodate someone else's belongings.

A little surprised, I thanked her for her help and asked, "How do you know my name if I didn't tell you?"

"Really? You didn't tell me?"

"No," I answered.

"So I guess that means that when you meet someone who is going to be your friend, you not only guess what they need, but even their name," she said, smiling.

Two minutes later, when I returned to my room to brush my teeth, I realized that my name was written on my closet and my bookshelf. I laughed, knowing that Claudia had read it as well.

When someone tries to lighten your afflictions—even without knowing you—and realizes your needs before you express them, a sense of gratitude comes to your heart. You feel calm from the moment you discover that you will not walk alone on a path you have never traveled, because someone who has already done it is willing to show you how to enjoy the journey. You do not need to be a fortune teller to know that this person will be an important part of your life and that her name will be forever written in your memory.

That morning I was grateful because one person knew that I needed someone to share my joys and sorrows, and without guessing ... I knew from that moment on that I had found that person.

45

WITHOUT LYING

After being married for over twenty-six years, my husband and I had the opportunity to make one of our dreams come true: visiting Hawaii. Of course, it was a week full of magic, where we could admire all the beautiful landscapes that we had often seen in magazines or on television.

As we arrived at the small airport on the island of Kauai, the climate made us feel at home. We had grown up in a place with the same characteristics, friendly people, humid air, and beautiful green vegetation. Everything we had heard and seen about Hawaii could not be compared to the reality we were living.

Before arriving at the hotel, we stopped at a coconut stand. The coconut water was delicious, and the pulp of the coconut was so rich that, at that moment, chocolate was in second place on my list of favorite foods. As we continued to drive on the narrow road toward the northern part of the island, we could not resist stopping for a moment to appreciate how wonderful it was to be in one of the world's most beautiful paradises. We admired the white sand beaches and the warm water reflecting that wonderful, blue sky. Knowing we would have plenty of time to explore and continue enjoying the island, we decided it was time to go to the place we would call home for the next week.

Three days later, we thought it was time to call home and check in with the children. Since we had arrived on the island, we had only sent text messages. We knew that because of the time difference, our children would most likely be asleep or at school while we explored the island. When I first heard their voices, I felt nostalgic, because for a very brief second, I thought that my trip would have been better if they could have joined us. However, they were well and enjoying being home without us, so my feelings of guilt disappeared.

We talked about the places we had already visited, such as waterfalls, caves, outdoor markets, and of course, beaches. "Mom, send us all the photos you have taken!" they demanded. We said goodbye, with the promise that we would send pictures as soon as we returned from the boat trip we had planned that afternoon. We would be able to have access to the part of the island that could not be seen by road.

I felt joy and freedom as I felt the warm wind on my face while I sailed in the open sea.

That night, I fulfilled my promise to my children and sent photos that described in detail the life we were currently living. I took the SD card from the camera and inserted it into my laptop. I smiled to myself, hoping that within all those photographs on the screen there were some that were decent. I wished that Ade and I had paid a little more attention to our daughter's instructions to know how to use the camera lens. I also remembered the words that my father had repeated so many times at home during my childhood: "The most important thing when taking a photograph is not the quality of the camera, but the photographer's eye."

I found some pictures that nice strangers had taken of us. Ade and I radiantly reflected the happiness and beauty that had overwhelmed us. After seeing that almost all of the pictures we took of each other were catastrophes, I began to regret not bringing at least one of our children along to be our personal photographer. Nevertheless, I kept my promise and sent a few photographs. I felt grateful that night because we still had a few days left on the island to capture better pictures.

Out of curiosity I opened my social media page and decided to change my profile picture. The moments we had enjoyed a few hours before on the boat had been wonderful, if only I could find the perfect photo ... And I found it. It was a picture that Ade took of me on the bow of the boat. The island was behind me with those emerald-green colors that make you think that the vegetation is unreal. The photograph also captured the magnificent sky and the incredible flashes of light in the waves. I appeared smiling, with a navy blue and white striped dress, which was the perfect combination of colors for that moment.

This photo was the one that best captured me, so I zoomed in on it only to realize with great disappointment that my eyes were closed and that my hair was a mess because of the wind. I quickly clicked to the next picture, hoping that it was a little better. Looking at the next photo, my hope began to disappear. It was the same pose, the same smile, and although the wind did not mess up my hair, the wind made my dress stick to my body in an unattractive way that displayed all of my love handles. At that point, I was almost sure that this photograph would not be the one I would show my family and friends, so when I skipped past that photo, I almost shouted with joy when I realized that my husband had had the inspiration to press the button on the camera not once, not twice, but three times!

The third photo captured the perfect landscape, my hair was in place, I had a radiant smile, my eyes were open and bright, and the soft breeze made my dress show off a beautiful silhouette. After having reviewed every single little detail, I finally had a new profile picture.

The next day, I sent some other photos home and uploaded a new photo to my social media page of a plant that grew in my childhood home. While on my page, I noticed that many nice comments were left on the picture I had posted the previous day.

For a moment, I felt like a fraud because I felt I was hiding who I really am. My imperfections had been hidden as I decided to erase any trace of that truth. I went back and looked at the three photographs side by side, and when I saw the differences, I could not help but laugh. No, I was not lying, because I am the same person in all three photographs. I am the one with the messy hair, the one with the dress that shows all of my body's imperfections, and the one in the perfect picture. I could not deny it: it was me in each of those shots. I simply decided to show the world my best self.

I saved two photographs that I have never looked at again. Even if I erase them, I know that they exist and show something of me that is not pleasant in my eyes or those of others. They are images that will always remind me that, although we all have traits or ways of behaving that are horrible, we must hide that unpleasant part of ourselves. Not because we are lying or trying to pretend to be somebody we are not, but because there is no need to show our flaws when we have the opportunity to show off our best side.

We do not lie when we display our best photographs that bring smiles and good comments from those who have had the opportunity to see our best self. We do not lie when we try to hide what makes us feel miserable, uncomfortable, or imperfect. We do not lie when we show the world our kind, gentle, loving, and helpful side. We do not lie when we try to erase those traits that show our insecurities, weaknesses, anger, or frustrations. We do not present a fake person when we decide to show just our moments of happiness.

Our life is the same as any photo shoot. There are photos and attitudes that are to be shared instantaneously, others that need to be retouched and edited before we share them, and some that need to be permanently deleted. If we have been seen at some of our worst moments already, we should not lose hope that we can replace those bad memories if we show something better.

46

YOU ARE...YOU

Even when my cell phone is in my purse when I receive a call, it is always hard for me to find it. I am certain it knows how to hide perfectly until the moment when there is no one on the other end of the line. One morning, when I found my small but invaluable treasure lost in the depths of my purse, I could see that a call had been missed. When I realized that the missed call was one I had been anxiously waiting for, I quickly, but nervously returned the call.

The voice that answered me sounded very friendly. Upon hearing my name, she explained that she would love for me to work with her. Although it was not necessary at this point, she wanted a copy of my résumé. I told her that during the interview, I was very clear about my situation. My work experience was almost zero, because I had spent every minute of the last twenty-five years in my role as a wife and mother. With a laugh, she told me that the decision to offer me the job was because of the skills that I had developed throughout my life, and that they were the ones that they needed at the moment.

At the end of the call, I looked at my friend and said, "They say that they want to hire me, but now I'm not sure I want to work eight hours a day, five days a week. They also asked me to write a résumé."

My friend smiled and said, "It's so simple! Just don't make your résumé more than one page, and everything will be fine. But before accepting the job, think carefully if that is what you really want to do."

I knew that my feet were firmly on the ground, because I was walking up and down the store's aisles, but my mind was worlds away. Thousands of thoughts concerning my résumé rushed through my head. I was mentally writing and revising a résumé while shopping.

I have had several opportunities to read résumés; I helped my husband, my son, and some of my friends put them together, so I knew what it entailed. But now, I personally understood how hard it is to describe yourself on paper.

I forgot about my troubles for a few hours while we shopped, but time had passed so fast since receiving the call that my friend and I realized it was past lunchtime. Not only were our feet tired from shopping, but our stomachs growled. We decided to stop at a small restaurant to continue enjoying the nice day.

We savored a delicious lunch. After all, Italian food was our favorite. After finishing the dessert, we stood up from the table and started walking toward the exit. At this time, I realized that a man was staring at us without trying to be sneaky. My beautiful blonde friend hurried out the exit, while I smiled at him and slowly headed for the door. However, the man stood up and almost blocked my path to the exit. The man continued to stare at me, so I asked, "Can I help you?"

He replied abruptly, with an unfriendly voice, "Are you from here or from Mexico?"

The question took me by surprise, but I answered with a firm "Yes."

I just heard him say, "Oh!" while he continued to stare at me without saying a word, so I quickly left the restaurant. I hadn't lied, because I have been living in this country more than half of my life, even though I was born in Mexico. My answer was yes to both questions, but I hurried out knowing that at the time, some people felt that being from other countries, especially from Mexico, means that you are not good.

When I got into the car, I told my friend what had happened. She let out a loud laugh when I told her that if she had not left the restaurant so quickly, I would have told the man that we both came from Mars.

At home, I was reunited with the people I had happily shared the last twenty-five years of my life with. We sat together in the kitchen while we talked about our day and decided what dish we would prepare for dinner. After preparing our meal, my children began homework while we waited to eat with their dad, who would return from work in thirty minutes.

My concerns about writing the résumé came rushing back. I still had no idea how I was supposed to fill an entire page with my personal information and almost nonexistent professional experience. But after thirty minutes, I finished a full two pages. I described myself to people who would know me only through what I wrote on those two pages. I mentioned the education that I had obtained in another country, the experience I had working for two years in a company before getting married. I was sure to mention that I spoke Spanish and that several times I had been a guest speaker at some conferences. I wrote about all the volunteer work that I gave through the years, and I didn't forget to specify my expectations. When I reread the pages, I almost laughed because the person being described was a stranger to me.

At the dinner table, I explained with more detail my experiences from the day, and I asked my family if they could describe me in one word, what would it be?

"Determined, motivational, mom, Mexican," were the words that they said. At the end, we all laughed when we heard the youngest of our family say, "I can tell everyone that you are *you*."

All the details in our lives—our résumés, height, hair color, languages we can speak, where we were born, or the titles that we have obtained—are not important to those we love. It does not matter as long as we continue to be the person they can trust, who cries with them in moments of pain, who they can laugh with, and who always celebrates their achievements.

I do not need to describe to my loved ones who I am or where I come from. What we write on a piece of paper will not change who we are. You cannot make your family see your qualities or abilities just because you described them on a page. That is not going to make us look better, more respectable, more capable, or wiser in their eyes. They already know who you are, and you are you.

ABOUT THE AUTHOR

Rosie Martinez was born in Mexico and moved to the USA when she got married. She started writing stories when she noticed her journal was repetitive because her days were so similar and common. She decided to find a lesson in every situation and turned it into a story with a moral to share.Since she turned 13 years old, she was invited to share in public some of her stories. Even when she studied Chemistry, she found a way to invite the people to look for the bright side in any circumstance. She lives in Utah.

amomentinmyhands.blogspot.com

Made in the USA
Columbia, SC
09 March 2018